Performing Under Pressure is written from the unique perspective of a man who trains some of the world's top athletes and executives to excel. It is about experiencing more success — with less stress.

Drawing from his experience as a high-profile performance and sports psychologist, and business consultant, Dr. Miller describes the numerous strategies that assist the PGA golfer, the NHL goalie, the NFL linebacker and the Olympic athlete as well as the executive, the salesperson, the actor and the student. He offers insights on how to enhance concentration, control, programing, personal power and the psychological technology for less stressful living.

Sport is the metaphor. There is no area with a clearer, faster bottom-line that's more high pressure than world-class sport. Using examples from sport and business, Dr. Miller elaborates on how the same training methods that enable a major-league batter to be more focused and aggressive towards the ball can help the corporate manager or professional to be more focused and effective under pressure.

The key to maximizing your performance.

———————

"I brought Saul in to work with the Mets because it is important to have a clear mental picture of what you want to do, to relax, and to be able to concentrate. That's what he teaches. I wanted him to communicate that to some of our players, and he has."

~ **Davey Johnson**
  Manager 1986 World Champion New York Mets

"The work I did with Saul helped me in turning things around. I'd recommend his approach to anyone."

~ **Ray Knight**
  All-Star third baseman, Cincinnati Reds, N.Y. Mets
  The Most Valuable Player, 1986 World Series

"Saul showed me a good technique for relaxation and breathing. He tuned me in to the waves of power. It's a good way to be calm, effective, and powerful."

~ **Sid Fernandez**
  All-Star pitcher, New York Mets

"Dr. Saul Miller has some fascinating ideas about relaxation, breathing, and focusing. Saul taught me how to focus my energy while I was on the field. The two years we worked together were two of my best."

~ **Jim Beattie**
  Former pitcher, Seattle Mariners
  Head of Player Development, Seattle Mariners

"You face some pretty intense situations as a short-reliever in the major leagues. And there are techniques that will help you to perform in those high pressure situations. Saul's got them. If you ever have to perform under pressure, I'd highly recommend you read the book."

~ **Matt Young**
  Pitcher, Boston Red Sox

"Saul's helped me to stay tuned into the winning channel no matter how much static there's been around."

~ **Johnny Johnson**
  NFL All-Pro safety, Los Angeles Rams

"A successful business is very much like a winning sports team. When I met Dr. Saul Miller I was impressed with the work he had done as a performance consultant to the New York Mets, the Los Angeles Rams, and a number of Olympic teams. Saul has now been working with me and my top managers for over three years and the results have been far better than I expected … now with Saul's help we are a better team. We play the game with more focus, more efficiency, and more ease. Saul's contribution has been significant and appreciated."

~ **Clark Higgins**
  President, Corona Clipper Company

"Dr. Saul Miller is an energetic, positive, performance coach. He's had a very positive impact on our team, our programmes, and our ability to cope with the pressures of providing and selling quality service."

~ **Sandra Routledge**
  Vice President, The Columbia Center

"Saul has a practical sense, know how, and the ability to communicate. In the past couple of years his work has made a significant difference for some of our players. If he can relate just a part of what he does in his book, it will be well worth reading."

~ **John Robinson**
  Head Coach, Los Angeles Rams

Over the years I've seen a number of books on winning and overcoming stress. Some make interesting reading, but what's interesting isn't always practical or effective under *real* pressure. I know. For the past thirteen years I've been a goalie in the National Hockey League.

I don't think there are many jobs more high-pressured and more stressful. One of the great goalies once said, "Imagine a job where every time you make a mistake a red light flashes on behind you and thousands of people cheer." It's intense. Something that's helped me to cope with the game, the playoffs, the injuries, the trades and to stay focused and excel in spite of it all is that I've been using Saul's techniques for years. They've made a tremendous difference to me. I'm more effective and have a lot more fun because of the knowledge Saul shared with me.

In pro sport, life at the top can be very short. The average is about three years in the NHL, NFL, and in major league baseball. The work I did with Saul has added years and enjoyment to my career.

Performing Under Pressure describes an approach that really works. In the book, Saul tells of his experience working in the NHL, NFL, major league baseball, the Olympics and with corporations and people around North America. The way he describes it is the way he does it. Saul has distilled the essence of some powerful techniques from different disciplines and he presents it here in a clear and entertaining style.

Winners in any field frequently have to react under pressure ... and in a second. The techniques described in this book will help you to do that. Whatever you do and whatever you want to do, I'm sure you'll find this book a useful and entertaining experience. I highly recommend it.

Glen Hanlon
Detroit Red Wings
NHL All-Star

I've used Dr. Miller's techniques for six years, through two Olympics, and in winning two Pan-American gold medals ... and they're great.

In *Performing Under Pressure* he describes what actually works in competition. His "breathing keys" are unique and powerful. His techniques for releasing, streaming, clearing the screen and "changing channels" are all tools you can use under pressure. And his insights and suggestions for refocusing thoughts, images and feelings have been very helpful to me. Ideas like, "it's easier to be aggressive than to hold on," "pain is power," "I deserve to express my ability" and "I control the switch," are all thoughts that have made me a winner.

The approach Saul uses and describes in *Performing Under Pressure* is really effective. Take it from me. I've worked with it. It won't just give you an edge in playing your game ... it'll help you to win in every aspect of your life.

Patrick Burrows
Canadian Olympic Team 1984, 1988
Two-time Pan-American gold medalist

PERFORMING UNDER PRESSURE

SAUL MILLER

McGraw-Hill Ryerson
Toronto   Montreal

*To all of us who strive and press to excel, to win, to be at our best ...
and to be loved.*

First published in 1992 by
McGraw-Hill Ryerson Limited
300 Water Street
Whitby, Ontario
L1N 9B6

1 2 3 4 5 6 7 8 9 0 RRDH 1 0 9 8 7 6 5 4 3 2

ISBN 0-07-551292-0

Canadian Cataloguing in Publication Data

Miller, Saul (Saul B.)
     Performing under pressure

ISBN 0-07-551292-0

1. Stress management. 2. Success. I. Title

RA785.M55 1991   155.9′042   C91-094439-3

Printed and bound in the United States of America

TABLE OF CONTENTS

---

section one:
INTRODUCTION   1

---

chapter one
WE ARE ALL PERFORMERS   6

The challenge to excel affects us all. Many of the same techniques that have helped some of the world's top performers can work for anyone … anywhere.

chapter two
PRESSURE …   12

A look at pressure: what it is, what produces it and what it feels like, plus an introduction to the two basic approaches for transforming pressure and stress into success.

chapter three
FORMULA/STRATEGY   24

"The mind is like a TV set that watches one program at a time, and you control the switch. If you don't like the program, if it doesn't empower you or give you pleasure, change the channel. It's your TV." An important part of performing under pressure is learning how to change channels and developing quality performance programing … and doing it without drugs.

section three:
RELEASE 83

It's seemingly simple but true. The ability to release (excessive) tension and limiting thoughts is basic to consistent high-level performance. This section is all about … releasing.

chapter eight
THE RELEASE REFLEX 85

Here is a perfect balance to the natural, defensive, reflexive tendency we all have to contract and tighten up under pressure. The "release reflex" is especially valuable when you want to excel in highly stressful environments.

chapter nine
TENSION RELEASE AND SCANNING 94

Learning to breathe and release tension is a simple, effective way to teach people to "control the switch"… and "clear the screen." An initial, temporary tension-release process is followed by a three-second technique for staying loose and being more effective.

chapter ten
STREAMING 115

Energy can be channeled or streamed through the body to strengthen your natural ability. Streaming is a powerful technique to enhance performance and reduce stress and pain.

chapter eleven
BLOWING OFF TENSION 131

It is stressful and unproductive to habitually suppress your feelings. In this chapter we describe an expressive, assertive way to free and empower performance.

chapter twelve
INDIVIDUAL DIFFERENCES 139

Everyone has a different optimal performance range. While each of us can benefit from learning how to release, some people perform better when they are more highly aroused than others.

chapter thirteen
CHANGING CHANNELS 155

"What channel are you on?" A summary of how to change channels on your mental TV and a reminder of the importance of developing winning programs.

section four:
REFOCUSING 167

Performing Under Pressure is about combining a technology for ease and optimal arousal with being more aware, focused and directed. The section looks at winning programing: high-performance images, "power thoughts" and feelings of competence.

chapter fourteen
HIGH-PERFORMANCE IMAGERY 169

Imagination is one of the most powerful qualities of the mind. Three different kinds of high-performance imagery are described along with ten principles for using your imagination to shape your reality into one of more ease and more impact.

chapter fifteen
SELF-TALK AND POWER THOUGHTS 196

Most people think over 50,000 thoughts a day. What we think and say to ourselves has a profound effect on how we perform and feel. This chapter explores the power of positive thought and self-talk, and provides coaching directives and examples that will enhance performance and wellbeing.

chapter sixteen
FEELINGS OF COMPETENCE AND CONFIDENCE 214

Part of excelling under pressure is using your mind to create feelings that empower you, that reinforce a sense of competence and that build your confidence.

PREFACE

Performing Under Pressure is about my experience training some of the world's top performers and how *you* can use the same techniques to enhance your performance and wellbeing in whatever you do.

Performing Under Pressure is a notebook on winning, developing potential, and increasing resistance to stress. And it's about doing it naturally. Too frequently these days, people look to magic potions to help them perform or deal with their stress and dis-ease. In sport, business, entertainment and the professions, biochemistry has become the source of the quick fix, or "the silver bullet." The problem is that drugs (including the "uppers," energizers, strengtheners, steroids, beta blocks and tranquilizers) aren't safe or effective ... and they nurture dependency. In our performance-oriented, "bottom-line-conscious" society, we need to devote more time and energy to educating and training people, especially our youth, in a *psychological* technology that will enable them to increase success, reduce stress and have more awareness and control. It's important we begin now.

Performing Under Pressure is a how-to book. It provides insights on enhancing concentration, control, focus, attitude ... and personal power. Each chapter contains specific training techniques and a number of illustrative examples. As you read through the examples and techniques, I encourage you to work with them and adapt them to your lifestyle and to your own personal quest for excellence.

I hope you enjoy the book, and that it contributes to your greater productivity, health and happiness.

Saul Miller

ACKNOWLEDGEMENTS

I would like to express my gratitude to everyone who contributed to *Performing Under Pressure*: to Glen Ellis for his enthusiasm, perseverance and creative input. To his colleagues at McGraw-Hill Ryerson: Susan Calvert, Heather Lange, Hania Fil, and Heather Somerville for working to create something special. To Susan Kerr for some excellent constructive feedback. To Perry Goldsmith, Lawrence Cooper, Michael Goldberg, Sherry Robb, Ted Mason, Morris and Anne Miller, Sharon, Paul, and Mitchell Wolfe, Keiko Takehashi, and Stan Hodson for their encouragement and support. To Leonard Orr, Marjorie Barstow, Walter Carrington, Dr. Edmund Jacobson who shared insights on breathing and easing up. To Laara for pointing out some directions and landmarks over the years and for insisting I do it on my own ... and to Garfield who inspires my best.

I would also like to acknowledge some of the coaches I collaborated with. The list includes: Davey Johnson, John Robinson, Roger Neilson, Harry Neale, Pat Quinn, Vic Rapp, Jim Poling, Gary Meredith, Mike Murphy, Bud Harrelson, Gil Haskell, Bas Lycett, Ron Hayman, Des Dickie, Shiv Jagday, Ron Polk, Mike Campany, Clark Higgins, Bruce Johnson, Pavel Katsen, Rene Lachemann, Mel Stottlemyre and Daniel St. Hilaire; the administrators who supported my involvement, most notably: Joe McIlvaine, Fred Claire, Dan O'Brien, Rogie Vachon, Frank Cashen, Carl Scheer, Victor Warren, Bob Ackles; the medical staff and trainers: Drs. Jack Taunton, Toby Friedman, Clyde Smith, Ron Madison, Steve Garland, Larry Ashley, Peter Demers, Garrett Giemont. And most especially, the many high-pressure performers that it has been my pleasure and good fortune to consult with: Jim Asmus, Gary Athans, Marie-Claude Audet, Bill Bain, Kevin Bass, Steve Bauer, Jim Beattie, Russ Bollinger, Cindy Bortz, John Brenner, Dieter Brock, Pat Burrows, Bruce Castoria, Gary Carter, Mark Carreon, Chris Coberstein, Jim Collins, George Crosier, Julio Cruz, Quentin Dailey, Eric Dickerson, Don Dougherty, Bobby Duckworth, Lenny Dykstra, Ricky Ellis, Sid Fernandez, George Foster, Jim Fox, Mark Fuller, Gary Galley, Paige and Megan Gordon, Anders Hakansson, Glen Hanlon, Mark Hardy, Curt Harnett, Dennis Harrah, Dale Hatcher, Ed Hearn, Ken Howell, Rick Honeycutt, Tom Horrell, Tony Hunter, Leroy Irvin, Gary Jeter, Mark Jerue, Howard Johnson, Johnny Johnson, Jeff Kemp, Ray Knight, Mike Lansford, Rick Lanz, Duval Love, Nancy Lopez, Tony Lopez, Morris Lukowich, Ed Lynch, Dave Mackey, Kevin McCarthy, Rollie Melanson, Alain Metellus, Randy Meyers, Hugh Millen, Garfield Miller, Kevin Mitchell, Peter Milkovich, Don Mundie, Jim Nelford, Jim Nill, Damen O'Hagen, Mel Owens, Joe Paopao, Pat Putnam, Larry Playfair, Reg and Stanley Plummer, Barry Redden, Doug Reed, Gervais Rioux, Ross Rutledge, Joe Sambito, Ron Shusett, Jackie Slater, Doug Smith, Stan Smyl, David Spears, Mike Stanton, Alex Steida, Karen Strong, Jenny Susser, Roy Thomas, Yvon Waddell, Brian Walton, David West, Dave "Tiger" Williams, Doug Yeats, Matt Young, Michael Young, Jack Youngblood, Richie Zisk, Dick Zokol ... and many others. Thank you all.

INTRODUCTION

———

The mind is like a TV set.
It watches one program at a time.
And you control the switch.

If you don't like the program,
if it doesn't empower you
or give you pleasure,
change the channel.
It's your TV.

chapter one

WE ARE ALL PERFORMERS

———

In principle, it's really quite simple.
Excelling is about having a clear idea of what you want to do …
and acting on that idea.

However, sometimes something comes between the desire and the doing.
That something is often pressure.

It was great drama. It was the sixth game of the World Series, and the New York Mets were trailing the Boston Red Sox three games to two. It was the tenth inning and the Mets were losing five to three. There were two out and two runners on base. One more out and the Mets would lose the World Series.

The Mets' batter stepping up to the plate was Ray Knight, one of the more competent and competitive players in the game. And like many competitors, in his desire to excel he'd sometimes try too hard, tense up, and this interfered with his performance. As he stood at the plate facing the pitcher at that critical moment in the game and the Series, he desperately wanted to get a hit, to express his ability, to keep things alive. The Mets fans were frantic. The atmosphere in Shea Stadium was electric. The pressure was enormous.

It was pro sport at its best. With just one second left in the game and his team losing 29-27, Jim Asmus stood poised to kick a 33-yard field goal. The field goal would mean victory. Missing the kick would mean losing the game and probably this job.

It was a seemingly routine kick. The kind he had made at practice over 100 times during the week. However, the previous Sunday he had missed two short field goals and was blamed in the press for his team's loss. Now he stood in front of 50,000 people ... millions more on national television. The game and his job hung in the balance. The pressure was enormous.

The scene was the cycling velodrome at the summer Olympics in Los Angeles. It was the one-kilometer race, the fastest cycling speed race of them all. Three laps around the track, full speed against the clock. One chance, no repeats. The fastest time wins. Curt Harnett was only nineteen years old, the youngest in the race. He had been training for years for this moment. It's what he had dreamed about.

The whole race would take less than sixty-five seconds. The question was, would he be able to bring it all together ... his desire, talent, training and technique? As his turn approached, he could feel the tension building and his heart pounding. The pressure was enormous.

The batter, the kicker and the cyclist are my clients, along with many other outstanding performers. The list includes major league All-Stars, NFL quarterbacks, NHL goalies, tour golfers, Olympians in a dozen different sports, as well as stock brokers, surgeons, writers, actors, musicians, managers, dentists, lawyers, and people in marketing, sales, movie making, rehabilitation and law enforcement. Most are highly motivated. They *want* to succeed, to win, to realize their goals. In so doing, they repeatedly face the challenge of having to perform and excel under some intense, high-pressure situations. At one time or other, all of them have had tension, pressure, anxiety and stress alter their perception, undermine their confidence, affect judgment and limit their performance.

My job is to facilitate success. I help my clients excel. To do this, I work with both mind and body. I show them how to exercise more psycho-physical control, and how to release tension, fear, worry and limiting thoughts. I also enhance their ability to "use" the situation, any situation, to tune in and focus on thoughts, images and feelings that give them power ... and then to express that energy effectively.

In the cases of the batter, the kicker and the cyclist, I spent hours working to help them to excel in just the kinds of intense situations I have described. Our goal, even under the extreme pressure, was to regulate their emotion, "change channels" and experience more ease, power and impact. And they did.

Ray Knight got the game-saving hit. The next night, he did it again. His home run in the seventh and final game of the Series was the decisive blow. He was the Series' most valuable player.

Jim Asmus made the field goal. His team won the game. In the two weeks that followed, he set two league records.

Curt Harnett rode a great race, a personal best. He recorded the fastest time of the day until the last rider surpassed it. He won an Olympic silver medal.

The most responsive and successful of my clients seem to share one quality. They have a clear idea or vision of what they want to do, and they are motivated to excel.

Sport has been my principal focus for much of the past ten years. I see it as a fascinating forum of human potential, a model of performance under pressure and a metaphor of life. It's an exaggeration, a drama and a game. Yet, in many ways, it's similar to what we all experience in our daily lives.

WE ARE ALL PERFORMERS

In the games of life we play, in our careers and relationships, in our challenges to excel, the pressures we experience can be very real and very intense. Most of us strive to be effective, powerful performers ... and to be fulfilled. Like the professional athlete, our performance and wellbeing can be significantly limited by tension, stress, anxiety, overeffort and negativity. A key to our productivity and pleasure is our ability to bring more ease and power to the moment, and to develop and maintain a clear, winning focus. That's what this book is about.

chapter two

PRESSURE

———

The high-performance mind operates at both an instinctive and a highly conscious level. At the instinctive level, it serves as an energizer … transforming impulse into action, receiving incoming (sensory) messages, relaying them and firing outgoing (motor) responses. The instinctive brain is an action brain. It doesn't think, it simply reacts. With the higher conscious mind, we set goals, analyze, interpret, image, affirm, reason, adjust and respond.

When we're performing well, there's an amazingly effective and complex interplay between these two levels of mental function. However, there are times when we get frightened, "nervous," and tense up, when the conscious mind overanalyzes and overreacts to incoming messages, when we think too much, say negative things to ourselves and interrupt the smooth flow of input to output. There are times when we try too hard, ignore our intuition and worry about the things going wrong instead of focusing on being effective and enjoying the moment.

One of the most frequently used terms to describe both the cause and the symptoms of this kind of performance dis-ease is *pressure*.

"What is it?"
"Where is it coming from?"
"Is it inside you ... or outside you?"
"Who creates it?"

I was seated in the office of the vice president of sales of the Corona Clipper Company, a quality garden tool manufacturer in southern California, with whom I'd been consulting for five years. The vice president was interviewing for the position of regional sales director and asked me to sit in. The man being interviewed was an experienced, successful salesman. Still, it was an important career meeting for him and he was nervous. His response to the pressure of the interview was to talk too much. He felt uncomfortable, and what he was attempting to do was to fill his uncertainty with sound, to "make a good impression." So he talked ... and talked. In so doing, he presented himself poorly. He would have been far more effective if he simply had taken a breath and released some of the fear and tension he was feeling, to have done something that enabled him to feel better about himself ... and be more calm and clear.

When the salesman left, the vice president asked me, "What do you think?"

"I think he talked too much," I replied.

"Way too much," he said. "If he gets the job, you'll have to do some training with him."

The man didn't get the job.

There are many people whose response to pressure is to push too hard, to talk too much ... or, alternatively, to contract and withdraw from expressing their full response-ability. Either way, they are operating from the effect of the fear and pressure in their lives. Either way, the result is that they reduce their effectiveness and pleasure.

Pressure isn't having to make the putt to win a big money tournament. It's having to make the shot when you've got $20 on the match ... and only $5 in your pocket.
~Lee Trevino

Pressure is a feeling of dis-ease that is inextricably linked with motivation and the desire to be or do *something more*. Pressure is about being attached to outcome, about really wanting to make something happen ... and feeling just maybe I can't. It's about pressing to meet the expectations of others ... which, again, is wanting to be something more. It's also about struggling to avoid the fear, pain, disappointment and embarrassment you associate with failure.

It's pressure that visits the golfer close to the lead when he suddenly loses his touch on the last few holes. It's pressure that gives the young pitcher the uncomfortable sensation that the plate is moving. It's pressure that robs the speaker of his confidence and ease as he stands before the audience he's about to address. And it's pressure that causes the actor to blow his lines in audition, the salesperson to press too hard and the student to "go blank" in an exam.

Pressure is pervasive. It's not confined to the obvious "test situation." It can follow you anywhere: into career, relationships and quiet moments by yourself. It's there when you are struggling to get ahead, and to make ends meet. It's there when you are concerned about saying and doing the right thing, and about being accepted. And it's there when you reflect on the meaningfulness of your life.

THE SEMINAR

I am standing in front of a mixed business audience of about 250 people giving a seminar on performing under pressure. I begin by asking the group to imagine a scene. It's the same scene I presented at the start of the book.

"It's Shea Stadium and the sixth game of the 1986 World Series. The New York Mets are losing the game and the Series. It's the tenth inning and they're trailing the Boston Red Sox five to three. There are two out. It's the Mets' last chance. If the next batter is out, the Series is over and the Mets lose."

I pause for a moment ... "I want you to imagine that the batter stepping up to the plate at that critical moment in the drama is *you*." (There's some laughter.) "There are 55,000 people in the stands ... 55 million more watching you on television. You desperately want to get a hit, to come through. Imagine that you have the talent and the ability. The question is, what would you do in that high-pressure moment to help yourself be at your best? Even if you're not a baseball fan, please consider what you could do to perform under pressure."

After a moment, I continue, "The image may seem more dramatic and high-profile than what most of us experience in a day's work, yet in many ways it's about the very same fear and pressure. Each of us is an expert in creating pressure in our lives. I would appreciate you relating some of the things that cause you pressure."

The audience responds.

"Deadlines." (A favorite pressure stimulus.)

"Just the word deadline is pressure," I interject. "What does it mean? If you don't deliver the goods on time, you die? ... the project dies? ... the boss dies? Deadline is a frightening word."

People laugh.

"What else causes you pressure?" I ask.

"Being successful in my career," says a young woman.

"Quotas," volunteers another.

"What kinds of quotas?" I ask.

"Having to maintain a certain sales volume," is the reply.

"Working on commission."

"Having to ship so much a day," adds someone else.

"Pressure is meeting the goals I set for myself."

"It's speaking to large groups."

"It's accountability."

"Pressure is picking up the kids on time."

"It's having call-waiting."

"It's paying the mortgage."

"Making money."

Suddenly the audience is involved. This is about every aspect of life.

"Staying in shape."

"Being on time."

"Getting around Los Angeles in traffic is pressure."

"Being supervised can be real pressure."

"Especially if you work for more than one supervisor," adds someone else.

"It's rising production costs ... and trying to compete with the tide of cheap foreign imports flooding the market."

"Pressure is about trying to produce a better quality product for less money in less time."

"It's trying to be a good parent."

"Staying on my diet ... losing weight."

"Working for someone who's demanding and insensitive."

"Making a partnership work is pressure."

"It's trying to satisfy others."

"Pressure is playing to a five handicap."

"It's keeping up?" says an older gentleman.

"Keeping up what ... or with what?" I ask.

"Everything," he replies.

There's more laughter.

"Pressure is trying to make right decisions."

"It's keeping the home office satisfied, and off my back."

"It's getting the job I want."

"Getting along with the rest of the family when we're all operating on separate agendas."

"Making our incentive program work."

"Pressure is exercising patience dressing my three-year-old daughter when I'm already half an hour late for work."

"Two jobs can mean pressure," I remark.

"Pressure is keeping my job."

"It's getting everything done on time."

"Pressure is making the most of my life."

"It's satisfying others."

"Pressure is making enough money so I don't have to worry about money all the time."

The seminar continues ...

"The term pressure means 'to press.' As you can see, all kinds of thoughts, situations and demands press on us every day. For most people, the 'biggies' behind an intense desire to do well are: the need to feel good about ourselves, to meet the expectations of others, and a limited sense of time, talent or money.

To summarize, pressure is a feeling of dis-ease that grows out of an intense desire to be or do something more ... accompanied by the uncertainty and fear that we may not succeed.

Pressure is a personal phenomenon. Just as many different situations can trigger it. Pressure feels different to each of us. I'd like to ask you what pressure feels like to you. When you're not even close to being prepared ... and you're facing a deadline for a project with career-altering consequences ... when you're stuck in traffic and already late for an important meeting ... when you haven't closed a sale ... or gotten a hit in weeks ... when a bear is at the door ... when the mortgage payments look enormous. ... What does the pressure feel like to you?"

"It feels incredible," says a woman in the audience. "It makes me tense."

"Specifically where in the body do you feel the tension?" I ask.

"I feel a band of tension around my head," she replies. "I get headaches."

"I usually feel it in my neck and shoulders," says someone else.

"I tighten up and stop breathing."

"I reach for a cigarette."

"I feel it in the pit of my stomach," says another. "I can't eat."

"I eat too much."

"Pressure gives me backaches."

"When I'm under pressure, I grind my teeth."

"It makes me feel tense and irritable."

"What's the 'it' you're talking about?" I ask. "Is it the pressure in-side you or outside you? Does something out there actually cause this feeling of tension and dis-ease or do you create the sensation?

Unless you own your feeling," I continue, "it's difficult to create another feeling in its place. There's plenty of variation. Head, neck, shoulders, jaw, bladder ... and that's the feeling of pressure we're aware of. Pressure can also be subliminal."

A client of mine had been a police officer with the Los Angeles Police Department for eleven years. We discussed how he dealt with the pressure caused by the potential danger of each and every call. Imagine what it would be like to work at a job where each call you respond to has a potential for explosive violence ... and could be the last call you'll ever make.

He told me, "I didn't think that way. I used to say to myself, 'It'll be okay. There's nothing to worry about, nothing's going to happen. Just take it easy and do it right.' I thought that the danger of the job didn't bother me as much as all the supervision and the internal poli-tics. It was only after I retired from the force that I felt this tremen-dous weight lift off my shoulders. It was the pressure of operating on the edge all the time. And I hadn't even realized it was there."

Whether we are aware of it or not, what's fairly consistent is that under pressure we all contract, tighten up and prepare ourselves for fight or flight. The problem is, while that instinctive, reflexive pattern may be invaluable for survival in the wild, in many ways it's coun-terproductive to health and high-level performance in the complex, high-pressure, results-oriented society in which we live.

The effect of prolonged or excessive pressure is that we tense up and cut down our breathing. We move out of the present ... and start to worry about the future ("what'll happen if ... ") and the past ("I should or shouldn't have done ... "). Our sense of confidence, ease and being in control diminishes. Our thinking shifts from a positive, creative, "I am ... ," "I will ... ," and "anything's possible ... ," to a more fearful, defensive, "don't mess up ... ," "be careful ... ," and "just hang in there." All of which limit health and performance.

If excelling is a process of creating a vision of what you truly want to achieve and then acting on it, then pressure is a feeling that intrudes into the space between our vision of success and our actually making it happen.

A young man interjects. "The pressure you're describing is negative. I enjoy a little pressure. I like to think of it as a positive creative force."

"It can be," I reply. "Some pressure is not only enjoyable ... it's essential. In physiology and medicine, pressure is a necessary part of normal function. In the sexual response, the build-up and release of pressure is an integral part of the pleasure of orgasm. In the circulatory system, it's pressure that enables the blood to circulate through the arteries and veins. What are undesirable and dangerous are repeated and prolonged periods of excessive pressure. What we call high blood pressure. That kind of excessive stress is life limiting. The pressure we've been talking about is a similar excess. It's 'high life pressure,' and it's to living and performing what high blood pressure is to circulatory function.

Of course, there are the individual differences as to what constitutes optimal pressure. What is ideal for one individual may be too much for another. Relief pitchers, hockey goalies, field goal kickers, stock brokers, air traffic controllers, surgeons and police officers all repeatedly have to perform under what most of us would perceive to be tremendous pressure. The ones who perform consistently well and seem relatively less affected by this pressure either have a higher pressure threshold or have developed better techniques for dealing with it."

"What's the difference between pressure and stress?" a woman asks.

"The terms are often used interchangeably," I reply, "and they're similar in many ways. Originally, they both referred to physical forces, like air and water pressure, and the mechanical stresses operating on a structure like a bridge or building. These days, they're more commonly used to describe psychological phenomena. People talk about 'feeling the pressure,' or being 'stressed out.' "

The principal difference I see is that pressure tends to be somewhat more situational and time-specific. For example, it's the *pressure* that the kicker feels to make the field goal, or that is on the golfer to sink the putt. It's the *pressure* to close the sale, finish the job on time … and to do it right. *Stress* seems to be general and diffuse. We say it's more *stressful* to live in a big city. Stress is so pervasive these days it's even being used as a verb. Recently, I overheard a young woman in New York say to a friend, "Don't stress."

I don't think the distinction between pressure and stress is very important. What is significant is the pattern of pressure you experience … your awareness of the circumstances that create it … learning what you can do to regulate and reduce the pressure … and how to enhance your performance and experience less stress.

FEELING LESS PRESSURED

There are two basic psychological viewpoints about pressure and how to handle it. The more *psychodynamic* approach suggests that most pressure is a function of the way we feel about ourselves, and that we become more vulnerable to pressure when we lack confidence and self-esteem. From this perspective, it is our fear, specifically our fear of not being okay, that pressures us to be successful ... and to avoid failure. As we become more self-accepting and comfortable with who we are, we identify less with our goals ... and are less in *need* of having to achieve and succeed in order to feel better about ourselves. Less need means less pressure ... and often better results.

That's not to say we shouldn't be motivated, set goals and direct our behavior. Not at all. The psychodynamic orientation is simply that it's healthier to work from preference rather an from addiction. Addiction is about responding from need. "I *need* for this to happen [to get a hit, to close a sale, to be a better lover] in order to feel good about myself." It's having to fulfill the need, to avoid the fear that exaggerates pressure. In a sense, this approach implies that if you could accept yourself more fully, you would experience less anxiety, less tension and less inhibition, and you would be freer and better able to express yourself and realize meaningful goals.

From the psychodynamic point of view, the ideal "therapy" is one that provides the insight into who you are and helps you to become more self-accepting and less fear-full. As such, you become less in need of having to do something in order to *be* someone and less vulnerable to the pressure of extraneous influences. Therapy focuses on insight and self-acceptance rather than on performance. It asks why ... "Why are you pressing so hard?" "Why are you so concerned about impressing others?" "Why does success mean so much to you?" Therapy can be a lengthy process.

The second orientation is more *behavorial*. It addresses the specific behaviors involved in feeling pressure ... and provides how-to training. Specifically, how to release tension, how to change feelings and how to refocus thoughts and images that enhance performance and wellbeing. The ideal is to develop more psycho-physical control. That is, to have more focus, power and ease in situations that previously were "tensing" and limiting. In so doing, one can maintain a more positive vision ... and perform accordingly. Training focuses primarily on enhancing performance. It may produce lasting positive changes in attitude. It is usually brief.

Both types of therapy are valuable. People who lack esteem are more vulnerable to pressure. And they're inclined to be more affected by it. However, from the practical point of view, if you're about to address a business meeting ... make a significant financial decision ... take a test ... attempt a high-pressure golf shot ... if you're caught up in traffic and late for an important meeting ... perform ... surgery ... or ... to pay the bills ... if you're a police officer responding to a call ... if you're about to step up to the plate at that critical moment in the World Series ... or to attempt the game-winning field goal with one second to go and your job on the line ... what you're probably looking for at that instant is not some insight on who you really are, but rather something that will give you the feeling and focus that will empower you to excel *now*.

chapter three

FORMULA/STRATEGY

There are so many guys out there with the same ability,
so what's the difference between success and failure?
The difference has to be the player's mental approach
to the game.
~Matt Young, Boston Red Sox

I was talking with the head of player development for one of the major league baseball teams about doing some "coaching" in the organization. When he asked about my baseball experience, I presented him with a list of some of the baseball players I've had the good fortune to work with over the years. The list included:

Kevin Mitchell
Lenny Dykstra
Howard Johnson
Sid Fernandez
George Foster
Rick Honeycutt

Jim Beattie
Kenny Howell
Richie Zisk
Randy Meyers
Craig Jefferies
Joe Sambito
Ray Knight
Matt Young
Julio Cruz
Kevin Bass
Gary Carter

The baseball executive looked over the list. "Impressive. That's a very talented group of athletes." Then he added with a smile, "Are you the reason they're all stars?"

"Not at all," I replied. "But just having worked with those winners has taught me a great deal."

There's an interesting paradox in the competitive forum of professional and world-class sport. The more successful you are, the stiffer the competition and the greater pressure you'll ultimately have to face. Working with these players and helping them to excel at the highest level has shown me some very effective keys to mind-body control, and it's taught me something about people who create success in their lives.

Most of my clients are winners. They're successful performers looking for ways to increase their success ... and reduce their stress. One of the most basic ideas that I introduce to help them, and one I repeat throughout the book is:

The mind is like a TV set.
It watches one program at a time.
And you control the switch.

If you don't like the program,
if it doesn't empower you
or give you pleasure,
change the channel.
You control the switch.

A fundamental neuropsychological principle is that whatever stimulus you focus on becomes magnified in your perceptual field ... while all the other stimuli are reduced. The phenomenon is called *lateral inhibition*.

In practical terms, that means ...

A. If you're worried and if you reflect on thoughts and feelings that cause you anxiety (like failure, embarrassment, disappointment, pain and sadness), these thoughts and feelings become exaggerated and magnified in your consciousness.

B. In contrast, if (in spite of pressure, doubt and fear) you tune into and focus on thoughts, images and feelings of ease, power and excellence, these qualities are strengthened in your consciousness.

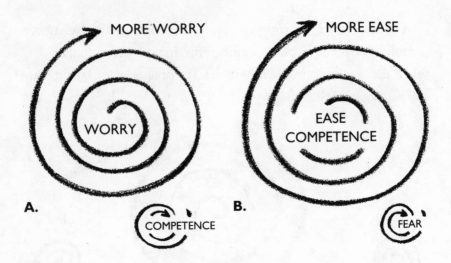

Something I've observed about consistent high-level performers is that they experience the same uncertainty, doubt, fear, anxiety and tension as everyone else. What's unique about them is that they don't dwell on negatives. Instead, they stay tuned into the power channel, to their vision ... and focus on empowering thoughts and feelings and getting things done.

One of the central ideas of performing under pressure is:

IF WHAT YOU'RE WATCHING DOESN'T

EMPOWER YOU ... OR GIVE YOU PLEASURE,

CHANGE THE CHANNEL.

IT'S YOUR TV.

YOU CONTROL THE SWITCH.

One way to develop your response-ability and strengthen a winning attitude is to enhance your ability to stay tuned into the power channel ... *even under pressure.*

A significant part of what I do in helping people to perform under pressure is showing them:

1.   how to "control the switch" on their mental TVs; and

2.   how to develop and tune into programs that give them power.

The idea of controlling the switch involves having psycho-physical control. By that, I mean being able to reduce tension and "arousal" levels and actually changing perceptions, feelings and thoughts. I do this by working with the breath, the body and the mind. These are the keys to being more alive and in the moment ... and to developing the long-term attitudes that nurture success.

"I want to feel like each batter I face is the pitcher."*

One Friday evening in early August at about 8:30, I received a phone call. It was from one of my clients who was a pitcher with the Los Angeles Dodgers. He was calling from the bullpen during the game, and I could hear the roar of the crowd in the background. We spoke briefly. He explained that one of his teammates who had not been pitching well wanted to talk with me. He put him on the phone. We spoke for a moment and arranged to meet early the next morning.

Saturday morning about 7:00 Rick arrived. He'd been a successful starter in the big leagues for almost a decade. Now he was struggling and in "a slump." He had experienced a string of "bad luck," and hadn't won a game in months. Instead of feeling confident and in command, this talented, experienced professional was feeling frustration and an intense pressure to perform.

We sat out on my back terrace. As we chatted, he explained that he was unsure of himself and wanted some help in regaining his confidence and focus.

"It's got to where I anticipate something going wrong every time I go out to the mound," he said.

In order to shift Rick's focus from being stressed to being positive, I asked him, "What is it that you want to experience when you're out there?"

"I want to feel like each batter I face is the pitcher," he replied.

I admired the way he put it, then I asked, "What are the specific feelings you have when you're really pitching great?"

---

*His comment was based on the old baseball saying that "pitchers can't hit."

He thought for a moment, then he answered clearly, "I feel loose. I move smoothly." (He got up from the sofa and demonstrated a certain movement for me.) Then he added, "Actually, when I'm really pitching great, I don't think much about mechanics. It feels easy, like I have time, and as if I can stretch my arm way out ... almost to the catcher, before I release the ball." I encouraged him to focus on these high-performance feelings and images rather than on the feelings of dis-ease and negativity that he'd been tuning in to under pressure. I assured him that as he gained more control over his emotions and was able to be more relaxed and focused, both his pitching prowess and his confidence would return ... and his luck would change.

To help Rick do this, I began by showing him three psycho-physical "keys" that related to his breathing. For the next thirty minutes, Rick sat back and focused on qualities of his breathing that he had never really experienced before. As he tuned into these keys, he felt more balanced, confident and at ease.

Next, I showed him a simple, effective process for releasing tension and stress throughout the body, something that would help him be more relaxed and in control and to express himself better. As we worked, he relaxed even more. Then I asked him to tap his creative imagination and to visualize himself pitching well, first in slow motion, throwing smoothly and with ease, taking time to stretch his arm way out ... to the catcher, before releasing the ball. Later, I asked him to imagine himself throwing with movement and velocity ("pop") on the ball.

With the imagery, I introduced the idea of using "power thoughts." These are specific thoughts that we put into our conscious minds to create and reinforce a desired behavior. The thoughts we used all went along with and supported Rick in feeling more at ease, more powerful and more in control.

Normally, it might take several sessions to accomplish what we did in those first two hours. However, Rick was a good student and we had incentive to move quickly. He was right in the middle of a major league season and it was possible he might be called on to pitch that very afternoon. Indeed, four hours after our first session he was performing in front of 40,000 spectators at Dodger Stadium, pitching in relief against the Atlanta Braves.

We had three more meetings that season, one at my home in Los Angeles the next day, and two at Rick's hotel in Montreal a week later. At each session, we spent time working with three basic elements — *breathing* and *release* techniques to generate more energy and flow and for greater psycho-physical control (to help Rick "change channels"). We also defined and *focused* on high-performance images and power thoughts to provide Rick with clearer, more effective programs to tune in to under pressure.

Rick was very responsive. I'm sure his success in the big leagues is as much a function of a good mind as a fine arm. Four sessions and eleven days after our first meeting, he made his first start in Philadelphia against the Phillies, and he excelled. He gave up only one run in seven innings and pitched himself out of difficulty. Throughout the game, he used his newly acquired pressure techniques to stay relaxed, focused and confident. He was back. After three years, he's still pitching well under pressure … excelling in the Championship Series and the World Series from 1988 to 1990.

Rick's story highlights some of the elements I've used to help hundreds of people to excel under pressure. Whether you're a pitcher, a putter or a pro quarterback … whether you're in management, marketing, service or sales, the same techniques apply. They are:

A. breathe B. release C. refocus

That's the formula we used in working with Rick, and it's the formula we'll follow in the book.

PSYCHO-PHYSICAL CONTROL

A great deal has been written about *the power of positive thinking.* To really put that powerful force to work for you and to enhance your ability to stay tuned into the success channel, I recommend that you learn how to regulate your emotions and develop more psycho-physical control.

By the way we're wired, almost every feeling we have is tied to and stimulates a thought. If the thought we are experiencing is strong, what I call a "power thought," it will stimulate an image. For example, when we experience a sharp sensation of pain, we automatically create a thought. The thought may be "Ow, that hurts!" "There's something wrong with me." "I can't do _____." Or "Relax, take it easy."

Under pressure the feelings we have are often charged with *fear.* The thinking and imagery these fearful thoughts stimulate is usually consequential and negative. ("What will happen if I don't _____?") The process of experiencing fearful thoughts, images and feelings increases pressure and stress, and it limits performance. Part of breaking the fear-pressure cycle is learning how to recognize those pressure feelings and to change channels on your mental TV. It's fundamental to consistent high-level performance.

The next two sections on **BREATHING** and **RELEASE** are about more psycho-physical mastery and learning how to change feelings of pressure into feelings of power.

BREATHING:
THE
THREE
KEYS
(WAVES
OF
POWER)

Did you ever notice what happens to your breathing when you're under pressure? If you're like most people, when things get intense, you tense up. You cut down your breathing, hold your breath or exaggerate the exhale process. And by doing this you limit yourself and heighten feelings of anxiety and dis-ease.

What's important to remember is that breathing is a powerful performance enhancer and a way out of worry overload. It's also a great balancing mechanism. You can use your breathing to "psyche up,"* calm down, improve your concentration, to recharge, "get it together" and be more in the moment.

When I'm with my clients, one of the first things I focus on is the way they breathe. It reflects the way they deal with tension and stress, and it's basic to how they feel about themselves … and how they perform. I've witnessed some remarkable performance shifts with clients who have learned to breathe with more ease and power.

Breathing is a psycho-physical bridge that connects mind and body. It's a great place to begin exercising greater awareness and control. The *breathing keys* I've found most helpful in maximizing performance and wellbeing are:

RHYTHM

INSPIRATION

CONTINUITY

Each of these keys is described in this section with examples and exercises that will help you to excel under pressure.

---

*The words "psyche" and spirit both have as an aspect of their original meaning the word *breath*.

chapter four

RHYTHM — THE WAVES NEVER RUSH

Rhythm is one of the organizing forces of the universe.
It creates order out of chaos.

In your personal life, one way to regulate your emotions and to empower yourself is to tune into the rhythm of your breath.

RHYTHM

Do you ever try too hard, especially when you really want to make something happen ... and notice that you're holding your breath, rushing yourself and tightening up?

The problem when we rush, overeffort and hold our breath is that we slip out of our natural rhythm. We become nervous, impatient and less effective.

At times like this, it's helpful to tune into the rhythm of your breath and remember, "The waves never rush."

The new Dodger pitcher was feeling the pressure of all that was expected of him. The fact that he grew up in southern California and was finally realizing his childhood dream playing for the Dodgers made matters even more intense.

"When I'm out there, it's as if my mind is running faster than my body," he said. To integrate the two, I suggested he tune into the rhythm of his breath.

"Your breath is like waves in the ocean," I told him. "Just as the waves never rush, don't rush your breath. As you breathe, give yourself time for your inbreath to come all the way in … until it becomes an outbreath. Give yourself time for the outbreath to go all the way out … until it becomes an inbreath. You deserve your time."

He tuned into his breathing rhythm. He experienced the inbreath come all the way in. He followed the outbreath all the way out. Almost immediately, he began to feel more balanced and at ease.

"What I've observed," I explained, "is that the fastest way out of disintegration and dis-ease is by tuning into the rhythm of your breath. It integrates the left and right cerebral hemispheres of the brain,* and it will enable your mind and body to perform more as one."

---

*The left and right cerebral hemispheres control analytic and coordination/intuitive functioning. When these hemispheres are performing in an integrated and synchronized fashion, performance and wellbeing are enhanced. Rhythmic breathing is a powerful integrative process.

One week later, the same Dodger pitcher was on the mound. He had been sent in at the start of the ninth inning to protect a one-run lead. There was one out and a runner on second base. The first month of the season had been a disaster for him. He had been charged with four losses and had an ERA* of 13.00 plus. Once again, he was in a jam.

His first pitch to the third batter was a beauty, on the outside corner of the plate. The umpire called it a ball. The pitcher could feel his blood pressure rise a few points. On the next pitch, the batter hit a ground ball to short, a routine out ... but the shortstop bobbled the ball. Now there were runners on first and third and only one out.

The pitcher tensed. He began thinking, "Not again ... five losses in one month would be devastating. I'm supposed to be the 'stopper' ... and I'm not stopping anything." The pressure of the situation, his terrible record, the bad call and the error all stimulated him to want to throw harder ... too hard. But more isn't always better. In pitching, it's called "overthrowing" (in sales it's "overselling") and it's a fear-based stress reaction that further limits performance. In the case of the pitcher, it had been part of his poor start to the season.

Suddenly, he remembered something we had been working on all week; when you feel like you're under pressure, *breathe*. He stepped off the rubber, and picked up the resin bag. As he went through the ritual dusting, he took a few slow breaths. With each breath, he gave himself time for the inbreath to come all the way in ... and time for the outbreath to go all the way out. It only took him four breaths to regain his composure. Then, feeling more focused and in command, he stepped back on to the mound, and struck out the next two batters for "the save."

---

*The average number of earned runs allowed by a pitcher in nine innings.

In the next few weeks, whenever he found himself tightening up and overefforting he tuned into his breathing. The simple technique of focusing on his breathing rhythm and giving himself time helped him turn his season around. He went on to win four of his next five decisions.

Another of my clients was a "pusher." He rushed and pushed at everything he did. He talked too fast, ate too fast and, by his own admission, made love too fast. His rushing was out of control and it interfered with both his performance and pleasure in life.

I observed him once at a sales meeting talking with a group of business associates. I noticed he was so intent on making his point that he stopped breathing. Characteristically, he was standing there holding his breath, poised, waiting to jump in. Seeing this, I got his attention and motioned him aside. I told him I was aware that he had something important to say. However, before saying it, I asked him to do a simple therapeutic exercise, just to breathe easily for six breaths. And with each breath to give himself time ... time for the inbreath to become an outbreath.

He did and visibly relaxed. Then I asked him, "Which is the real you? Is it the guy who's rushing and stressing himself, or the man who's breathing easily and looking good?" I reminded him that he deserved his time. He looked at me for a moment, took a breath, nodded his head and smiled.

In both cases, the pitcher and the salesman limited their effectiveness by trying too hard, tensing up and slipping out of their natural rhythm. Remember, one of the fastest ways of turning pressure and stress into a felling of power and ease is simply by tuning into the natural rhythm of the breath.*

The first breathing key is **rhythm**.

To experience the rhythm of your breath, take six breaths. With each breath, give yourself time for the inbreath to come all the way in. Give yourself time for the outbreath to go all the way out. **The key to rhythm is time.**

I tell my clients that the breath is like waves in the ocean. And just as the ocean waves flow in and flow out with a characteristic rhythm, your breath has a wave-like rhythm of its own.

~ Tune into the rhythm of your breath.
~ Give yourself time.
~ Allow yourself time for the inbreath to come all the way in.
~ Allow yourself time for the outbreath to go all the way out.
~ The waves never rush.
~ Don't rush the breath.
~ You deserve your time.

---

*As you read through this section of the book, take your time. Experience what's being said in relation to your breathing patterns. Parts of this chapter are written and paced to make it easier for you to be more in touch with your breathing rhythm … and to give you more time.

A sense of limitation can shape our thoughts and feelings. The sense that time is limited can cause us to rush and press. Pressing is stress and dis-ease.

Of course, the demands of life occasionally stimulate us to react quickly, and so we do. However, when rushing and pressing isn't just a momentary reaction but a way of thinking and living, then we slip out of balance ... and are vulnerable to stress and dis-ease becoming chronic, limiting, destructive patterns. Performance and health break down, and we "burn out."

A simple, effective beginning to preventing your adaptive reactions from becoming stressful, limiting habits is to repeatedly tune into the rhythm of your breath ... and give yourself time.

To do this, be aware that as you inhale you're allowing yourself time for the inbreath to come all the way in ...

Be aware that as you exhale you're allowing yourself time for the outbreath to go all the way out ...

Remember, the waves never rush.

Don't rush the breath.

There's power in taking your time.

Managing anything can be stressful. Managing a professional baseball team, like running a successful, competitive business or caring for a family, can mean months of almost continuous stress. In baseball, not only is the vigilance of the game intense and demanding, judgments can occupy time away from the field (office) and fill one's waking hours. When you add to that the *stress* of dealing with enormous egos, a large, aggressive press corps, and the second-guessing of thousands of rabid fans, it's easy to get so immersed in it all that you forget to breathe.

One day about halfway through the 1985 season, Davey Johnson, the manager of the New York Mets, asked me to show him something of the work I was doing with some of the players.* We had met several years before when Davey was managing at Jackson in the Texas League and I was teaching and consulting with athletes at Mississippi State University. Some of the baseball players I worked with at the time had really excelled. One tied the NCAA record for the most home runs in a single season, and another set a conference pitching record. Being both curious and innovative, Davey was interested in what I was doing to facilitate these athletes. A meeting was arranged. It was an interesting exchange of ideas and experience. Several years later, he brought me in to work with the Mets.

Now, still curious, Davey took half an hour out from the pennant race and a seemingly endless schedule, lay back on a sofa in his office and began to relax. With some guidance, he slipped into the rhythm of his breath. He experienced the breath as "waves" and gave himself time for the in wave (the inbreath) to become an out wave (outbreath).

After just a moment or two of breathing, he said, "You know, every once in a while in the ocean there's a bigger set of waves. It feels the same with my breathing. Every once in a while, say every seventh or tenth breath, there should be a bigger breath, a bigger wave." I acknowledged his intuition. There are no rigid patterns to breathing. The keys are rhythm, inspiration, continuity and what feels right to you. And slipping into his breathing rhythm and taking the occasional big breath felt right.

---

*See BATS by Davey Johnson, pp. 229–231 (G.P. Putnam's Sons, New York, 1986).

Davey's awareness of a sense of greater ease and power was apparent. After just a few minutes of breathing, he got up with a start. "Damn," he exclaimed. "I really haven't been breathing. Oh, I push myself to jog every day, but for me that's just more rush. This is simple enough and there's power in it. I could do with rushing less and breathing more."

Whether it's baseball or business, there are two things that can help a manager cope with stress. One is seeing employees performing well and "the team" being successful. The other is having a technique for effectively reducing pressure and dis-ease.

Something the Mets manager and some of his hitters discovered was that tuning into their breathing gave them more patience and enabled them to see more clearly. With just a few minutes of rhythmic breathing, you can begin to reprogram yourself out of a rush-and-struggle mentality into feelings of greater ease, power and confidence.

Don was a director of operations of thirty-two shopping centers on the West Coast. His job involved keeping 1,600 tenants and the financial group he served happy. If the power went off, if a pipe broke, if the weather was unseasonal, if vacancies increased, operational costs went up or sales dropped, Don heard about it. He experienced his job as a continuous pressure to keep things "right." What made things even more intense for Don was that he was a perfectionist who was forced to rely on hundreds of other people to get the job done. The sad reality was that many of these "others" were far less motivated and less involved than he was.

Don equated his job to that of managing a baseball team of high-priced individuals each with their own agenda and sensitivities ... and each with an eye on their own performance. He described how the monthly numbers his team posted (sales volumes, operational expenditures, vacancies and revenue per square foot) were equivalent to the numbers posted by a team of major leaguers (batting averages, earned runs and games won). When their numbers dropped, the pressure Don felt increased.

It's easy to tell someone to "ease up" and "don't let things bother you," Don remarked. "It's another thing to actually *be* more at ease and still be effective." I met Don after he'd had a heart attack, and along with recommending some significant, necessary changes in his lifestyle,* I counseled Don about his style of management.

Managing shopping centers is about managing people, time and space. That's a challenge. To give Don the sense of having greater control, I began by working with his breathing. I explained to him that while he couldn't control each and every situation, when it came to how he reacted he was the boss. In order to help him feel more like the boss, we focused on his breathing rhythm and experiencing the time he had available to him. That is, the time for his inbreath to come all the way in ... and time for his outbreath to go all the way out.

A key to psycho-physical control is pairing thought and feeling. As Don became more conscious of taking time to breathe, and as he experienced the feeling of the breath coming all the way in ... and going all the way out ... I recommended he think, "I'm the boss ... and the boss takes his time."

I encouraged Don to maintain this awareness at work and at play. I told him, "Whether you're talking on the phone, sitting in conference, walking the malls or reviewing numbers, you can always take

---

*The way we live each day is as important as what we can do at one moment to reduce pressure and stress. See Chapter 18 for lifestyle factors that nurture consistent high-level performance.

the time to breathe. Similarly, when you're exercising, eating, being social or playing golf, be conscious of experiencing your time: time for the inbreath to come all the way in. The boss takes his time."

Like many high achievers, Don was concerned that if he eased up his *performance* would go down. What he discovered was that taking time to breathe allowed him to perform or operate at a healthier and *more productive* pace. He was aware that his earlier perspective of rushing and pressing had contributed to his heart attack, and he was pleased with the change. "Now I've got the ultimate pacemaker," he said, taking a breath, "and it's me staying tuned in to the rhythm of my breath."

~ The first breathing key to performing under pressure is RHYTHM.
~ Rhythm is about using your time,
    allowing yourself time for the breath to change directions.
~ Remember, you're the boss ...
    and the boss takes his or her time.

~ Again, to experience your breathing rhythm, take six breaths.
~ With each breath, give yourself time for the inbreath to come all the way in ...
~ With each breath, allow yourself time for the outbreath to go all the way out ...
~ Don't rush the breath.
~ Don't force it or try to control it.
~ Instead, experience the rhythm of your breathing.

~ Tune into the rhythm of your breath.

~ There's power in rhythm.

~ The waves never rush.

~ You deserve your time.

A few suggestions on breathing:

It's almost always preferable to breathe through your nose. Energy is more easily and effectively processed by breathing through the nose than the mouth.

Allow *both* your chest and abdomen to be free to expand and contract as you breathe. And keep it simple. (Don't worry about whether your abdomen should expand before your chest, or your chest before your abdomen.)

Breathing with ease and power is not about taking large breaths. Once you've tuned into the three "keys," then you can increase (or decrease) the amplitude or size of your breath, according to the circumstances and the way you feel.

CHAPTER 4 TRAINING NOTES

The training suggestions at the end of each of the following chapters are for a four-week period. They are guidelines for you to work with to make the most of the techniques that are described in this book. It's not enough to simply read and "understand" the principles. The only way to really learn it is to do it.

Coach yourself. Work with the techniques. Adapt them to your circumstances, to your work, to the way you relate and recreate. Discover how you can best use and enjoy them to enhance your life.

Rhythmic Breathing

1. **Take a ten-minute "breathing session" every day.**

   As you do, tune into your breathing rhythm.
   Follow your inbreath all the way in ... until it starts to go out.
   Follow your outbreath all the way out ... until it starts to come in.
   Experience the rhythm of your breath.

2. **During week one**: At least two or three times a day, consciously take six breaths. Pick up your breathing rhythm. With each breath, give yourself time for the inbreath to come all the way in. Give yourself time for the outbreath to go all the way out ... and think, "there is time enough for me" ... or "the waves never rush." It's an excellent technique to remember when you're feeling rushed, or constrained. You can also give yourself more psychological distance, which will enhance your perception and your reactions to people and events around you, by simply

remembering to breathe … and thinking, *"I'm the boss,"* and "the boss takes his or her time to breathe."

3. I like to combine a feeling (the feeling of breathing rhythm) with a thought. Thoughts you can think with a client, in a meeting, or on the first tee include:

"There's power in rhythm."
"The waves never rush."
"I deserve my time."

It's advice I've shared with some of the planet's heaviest hitters.

chapter five

INSPIRATION — DRAWING IN POWER

From time to time, almost everyone experiences a little self-doubt. Under pressure, some people think the worst. They think "I can't," "no way" or "this is too good to be true." They operate as if there just isn't enough for them; not enough time, opportunity, luck or love.

The truth is, each of us has a personal connection to an unlimited supply of energy, power and good ideas. A simple, effective way to tap your power supply and to inspire yourself is to focus on drawing *in* energy and thinking of "things being possible."

Jim Lefebrve, the inspirational leader of the Seattle Mariners, is seen by many as a good coach and motivator. In Seattle, I've seen both players and fans wearing T-shirts saying, "I'm a Lefebrve Believer." And it's no wonder. Despite a history of losing, a young team, the toughest division in baseball, and one of the lowest payrolls in the game, Jim is making a valiant effort in turning the team around and making it competitive.

Lefebrve is a practical man who believes that under pressure people often make things too complicated by thinking too much.

One of his messages for performing under pressure is to *keep it simple*. As Jim puts it, "Simplicity brings security. Security gives you confidence. Confidence breeds consistency. And consistency means you can perform. It's that simple."

I agree with his philosophy. Under pressure, many people become too analytical and think and worry themselves into "a slump." Others perpetuate a slump by being hypercritical. One solution to worry and overanalysis is a simple psycho-physical response that provides a clear, positive focus. In effect, it's the essence of inspiration itself. It involves having people focus on the inbreath (the inspiration) whenever they feel pressured. Just that simple response enables them to re-establish their connection to possibility and to reaffirm their aliveness and direction.

I recall sitting in the dugout at the Seattle Kingdome talking to Lefebrve as he watched batting practice. I was saying that there was a link between being inspired and inspirational breathing, and suddenly he said, "Show me what you mean." So I did. I simply asked him to tune into his breathing. Then, I asked him to focus on the inbreath and on drawing/breathing in energy with each breath he took.

Thoughts can be inspiring, and to have a maximum impact they should exist in a context that nurtures inspirational thought. One way to create that context is to breathe … and with each breath to focus on drawing in energy and power. Part of inspiring yourself is realizing that you have a personal connection to an unlimited supply of energy and possibility, then drawing on that energy and thinking a positive thought. Each breath is really an opportunity to reaffirm our aliveness and direction. *You can inspire yourself with each breath you take.*

Being a goalie in the National Hockey League is about the most intense job in all of pro sport. You are the last line of defense ... and your mistakes are glaringly obvious.

Glen Hanlon is an All-Star, an eleven-year veteran goalie in the National Hockey League. We had maintained a relationship for years, first as client and counselor, then as friends. Going into the 1987 Stanley Cup playoffs, he wanted some input, something that might give him an edge, so he gave me a call. I reminded him of what we had worked on over the years: to stay in the moment ... to experience one breath at a time ... one shot at a time ... one period at a time... to see himself making the plays ... playing his angles ... stopping shots and being "like a cat." In essence, I reminded him of the basics: to breathe, to focus on the positive and that he was okay.

Glen split playing the first two series of the playoffs with the team's other goalie. Then his colleague was benched. With his team on the brink of elimination (down three games to one in the best of seven series), Glen was called upon to make a difference, and he played a great game. He recorded the team's first playoff shutout in twenty-one years. Two nights later, he did it again (the first two shutouts in a playoff series in thirty-five years). His team went on to win the divisional championship.

When I spoke to him about his performance the day after his first shutout, he said, "With about ten minutes to go in the game, I started to experience some doubt. I recall thinking, 'something's going to happen ... this is too good to last.' Then I noticed what I was thinking, so I took a breath. I inspired myself, and refocused on the positive. I thought of being 'like a cat,' playing the angles and being in the moment. After that, *I knew* I could stop anything." A moment later, he made another big save to preserve the shutout.

A more subtle, pervasive stress is the one we all face as players in a consumer society. For example, many of us are bothered by repeated unsolicited phone calls from salespeople offering "an opportunity" to buy something, or invest in some "high-yield," low-risk program that sounds like it can't miss. It's part of a constant background of noise and pressure that intrudes on us to buy more, be more and do more. After a number of these calls, it's not surprising that we often react to the next caller with less than a little patience ... unless we learn to *use* the disruption as stimulus to draw in energy.

What you are less apt to consider unless you've had some experience with "cold calling" is that on the other end of the phone the young broker selling the option has had his twenty-seventh straight "no, thank you" response. Instead of "losing power" and thinking "this is useless" or "I'm ineffective" (the kind of negativity that contributes to an over 50% attrition rate among stock brokers in their first year of business), he *uses* the rejection as a stimulus to take a breath. He consciously draws in energy, and *inspires* himself. Then he refocuses on the positive* and moves on to the next call.

The opportunity for turning what appears to be a frustrating stimulus into an empowering one exists in all relationships. Inspirational breathing can be a key. My wife does it all the time. I'll be waxing eloquent about something I believe to be very meaningful, really making a point ... or so I think. Then she'll look at me, consciously take a breath, draw in energy ... then change the channel.

---

*It's almost impossible to think positively when you're tense and holding your breath. The example is about using rejection and adversity as a reminder to breathe in energy and inspire yourself. After you breathe in energy, then refocus on a positive thought. (For more input on "power thoughts," see Chapter 15.)

The second breathing key is **inspiration.**

Inspiration literally means to take in spirit (or life energy). In this context, it means to focus on the inbreath ... on breathing in energy.

~ Each of us is surrounded by a limitless sea of energy.

~ With each breath, we can draw on that energy and draw in power.

~ With each breath, we can reaffirm our aliveness and direction.

~ With each breath, we can inspire ourselves.

~ Many people don't exercise that response-ability.

~ They look to something or someone else for inspiration.

~ Under pressure, people frequently tense up and lose power.

~ Their breathing becomes more shallow and limited.

~ Tension builds up.

~ And they release it with a "sigh of relief."

~ Then they go back to more limited breathing and the cycle repeats itself.

~ The problem with limited breathing is that it's low energy.

~ It can keep you down, locked into limited thinking and feeling, and operating from the effect of the pressure in your life.

~ Instead, focus on the *in*breath.

~ Focus on consciously drawing *in* power, on inspiring yourself and taking charge.

~ Then allow yourself to release and exhale.

Something I've noticed again and again is that when people are performing well they appear confident and relaxed. They breathe easily and naturally, and they don't think much about this process. However, when they're struggling or "in a slump" (any kind of slump), they usually tense up, cut down their breathing, worry and interfere with themselves. Shifting from a low- to a high-performance mindset becomes much easier when people remember to breathe and inspire themselves.

After a series of ailments and injuries, Ray Knight found himself struggling at the plate. As a former major hockey league All-Star, his lack of success caused him some frustration and embarrassment. He began to tighten up and interfere with his breathing, which only made it harder for him to see and react to the ball.

I did some work with Ray on his breathing. First, we focused on rhythm, on him taking his time ... then on inspiration, on breathing-*in* power. Ray picked up these two keys immediately. Then we added some high-performance imagery and power thoughts. As I said earlier, breath and thought go together. They are the fundamentals of human consciousness. Something that lifts performance is to pair a good feeling (an uplifting feeling) with a positive thought. Next, we worked at bringing this process to the "on deck" circle and to Ray's experience at the plate. The intention was, before Ray stepped to the plate, that he inspire or empower himself with his breathing and with some "power thoughts."

Learning is often a gradual process. Several weeks after our first sessions, I was sitting at home watching Ray on TV and noticed he was again tensing and pressing at the plate. Instead of breathing easy, he was holding his breath ... then pushing out the exhalation. Needless to say, he wasn't hitting the ball well at all.

I spoke with Ray at his hotel the following day and asked how things were going. He replied that for the past few days he hadn't been at all comfortable at the plate. "Are you feeling impatient?" I asked. "Exactly," he replied. "I'm not waiting for my pitch. I'm jumping at the ball...." Then he paused and asked, "What made you say impatient?" I explained what I observed was that he wasn't taking time to breathe and that he was pushing the outbreath. I told him that in my experience pushing the outbreath was often a sign of impatience. I reminded him that he knew what to do to take charge; namely, tune into his breathing, draw in energy and to affirm "I am ..." and "I will ..."

The story goes on. Fourteen months and half a dozen sessions later Ray was playing in the World Series. Following an outstanding season during which he had been one of the National League's top ten hitters, he began to struggle. In the Championship Series against Houston, he hit in the .160s. And he was hitless after game two of the World Series. Whether it was the pressure of post-season play, his intense desire to excel, great pitching or all three, Ray was again rushing himself, squeezing too hard and playing uninspired baseball.

I called him at this hotel room in Boston the morning of game three. As we spoke, he acknowledged his frustration and impatience. I reminded him of something simple and powerful; something we'd spent hours working on and something that would help him be calmer and more focused in front of 38,000 screaming fans in Fenway Park that night. I reminded him to *breathe*: specifically, to take his time and to focus on drawing *in* energy. With all the stimuli competing for his attention, his breathing would give him more patience. It would help him to relax and see the ball, not jump at it.

Following our conversation, his performance improved dramatically. He got a couple of hits that night, and he went on to hit .500 for the rest of the Series. In the first chapter, I described him coming to the plate in that critical situation in the sixth game. There were two out, two men on base and his team was losing by two runs. One more out, and they'd lose the World Series.

As Ray stepped up to the plate, he consciously focused on his breathing, and on drawing in energy. He moved out of the pressure and into a space where he could excel. He got the key hit, then a couple more, including a home run in the seventh and final game. He was the Series' most valuable player.

It's important that *you* experiment with the "breathing keys" for yourself. As you do, you may discover that "breathing" is not coincidental to consistent high-level performance. It's fundamental.

The same basic principles of giving yourself time … and empowering yourself … apply to all areas of performance. Salespeople, like athletes, can benefit by bringing more ease to their physical process and inspiring themselves. Nothing is more unpleasurable to a discriminating buyer than the feeling of being pushed by an impatient, overefforting salesperson.

Brenda's a good example. She was a commission saleswoman who sold with an "I've got to" attitude. Her desire to excel and her lack of esteem caused her to push and press too hard. Her pressing, in turn, caused the people she was selling to to contract and withdraw, and their withdrawal seemed to stimulate Brenda to press even more. The result was a high-tension, low-performance circle.

What Brenda required (and got) was more than just some feed-back on her sales technique. What we noticed was that she would cut down her breathing under pressure. So I spent a couple of hours working with Brenda on her breathing and her focus. What especially helped her was learning to take a breath and draw *in* power whenever she felt "challenged" or whenever she experienced the need to be acknowleged.

That simple response of replacing an aggressive surge with an in-spiration and the reminder, "I have a personal connection to an un-limited supply of energy," gave Brenda better perspective, more bal-ance and more ease. It allowed her to think of *service* and "What can I do for *you*," instead of *addiction* … "This is what I've got to have." The bottom line: Brenda began to feel more comfortable about her-self, and as she did her customers began to feel more comfortable. Her performance improved.

One of the most important things about sales is loving yourself and what you do. One way to experience more of that feeling is by learning to use your situation (any situation) as a stimulus for draw-ing in energy and inspiring yourself.

~ Shift your consciousness back to your breathing.

~ Experience your breath like waves in the ocean.

~ Notice that within each wave and each breath there's a balance.

~ Ideally, there's a gentle pull in against gravity followed by a more instant and free release.

~ When there's a free flow of energy, when we're relaxed, the
  wave flows smoothly.
~ We draw in energy with ease, and the outbreath looks after
  itself.

~ When there's tension and anxiety, we interfere with the wave.
~ We push, hold or force the breath.
~ We breathe too shallow and exhale too much.
~ All of this affects the quality of our thoughts and images,
  and limits our performance.

~ What's important to remember is that you have a personal
  connection to an unlimited supply of energy.
~ With each breath, feel yourself drawing on that resource.

~ Experience the inspiration for yourself.
~ Take six breaths.
~ As you breathe, focus on the inbreath.
~ With each breath, feel yourself breathing in energy.
~ With each breath, reaffirm your aliveness and direction.
~ With each breath, inspire yourself.
~ Then release.

Hitting a baseball, selling a product, performing a service and most complex activities require a balance of charge and release, or effort and ease. Overworking, tensing up, being impatient, pushing too hard may all be understandable symptoms of the high achiever, but when they interfere with natural response patterns like breathing they limit performance and wellbeing. One of the easiest ways of slipping back "into the groove" is by slipping back into the rhythm of the breath and drawing in power.

~ Relax and breathe.
~ With each breath, experience yourself drawing in energy.
~ You have a personal connection to an unlimited supply.
~ You can inspire yourself in everything you do.

CHAPTER 5 TRAINING NOTES

Coaching Inspirational Breathing

1. As you take your daily ten-minute "breathing session," feel yourself drawing in (breathing in) energy. First, pick up your rhythm, then focus on the *in*breath.

2. **Starting on week two**: At least three times a day, take half a dozen inspirational breaths focusing on the inbreath.

3. Repeatedly throughout the day, inspire yourself. Develop the habit, especially when you're feeling "stressed" or pressured, of going to the inbreath ... drawing in energy and *inspiring yourself*. Remember to use stress as a stimulus to draw in power.

4. Thought and breath work together. As you breathe, remind yourself:

   "I have a personal connection to an unlimited supply of energy."
   "With each breath, I feel more calm, more focused, more powerful."
   "I'm the boss."
   "I inspire myself."

Inspiring yourself is the beginning of exercising greater response-ability. Begin with this breath ... right now.

chapter six

CONTINUITY — THE WAVES KEEP ROLLING

I see the entire game as a series of waves consistently
coming in, never breaking stride.
~ LeRoy Irvin, All-Pro corner backer,
Los Angeles Rams*

Have you ever experienced a lapse or felt yourself losing your focus during an important meeting or event? Continuity is about order, direction and flow. One way to experience more continuity and consistency is to tune into your breathing.

**Los Angeles Herald*, April 12, 1986.

As a rookie for the New York Mets, Sid was a talented young pitcher who was somewhat erratic and easily upset. He wanted something to enhance his concentration and consistency, to help him to feel more relaxed *while* he was on the mound. We began by working with his breathing; the flow, the continuity and the thought that the waves never stop. Whatever was happening, I wanted Sid to experience that the waves keep on flowing. When he threw a great pitch, when he threw a strike ... there was the next wave. If he missed on a pitch ... there was the next wave. *Regardless of circumstance*, whether he was up by a run or down by three, whether he had walked the last batter or struck him out, the waves just kept on rolling. It was wave after wave, breath after breath ... and that flow was with him.

Over a period of three months, we spent eight or nine hours working together: on relaxing, breathing, experiencing the breath as waves in the ocean and relating that to his pitching. I encouraged him to tune into his breathing from time to time throughout the game. As a Hawaiian who loved the ocean, he enjoyed the wave metaphor and found it useful. The more he tuned into the consistency of the waves, the more ease and consistency he seemed to have on the mound. That year, the waves kept rolling as Sid led the major leagues in strikeouts per innings pitched.

Cam was a Mountie. He had been with the force for about ten years when he volunteered and was accepted to a "tryout training camp" for a Royal Canadian Mounted Police crack antiterrorist unit. This was a super-elite group, the best of the best, and selection meant surviving a grueling training process designed to "test" the candidates and push them to "the limit." Cam knew the camp would be rough going, so he sought me out for some psychological input that might help him endure the inevitable challenge ... and succeed.

We met only once for about two hours immediately prior to Cam's departure. In that limited time, I wanted to give him something that would be useful; something that he could actually apply under pressure. So I showed him how to use his breathing for greater continuity ... and to change doubt, negativity and a sense of "I can't" into something positive and productive.

Camp was brutal. One way to stress people and break them down is to exhaust them, to overload them physically and mentally and see if/where cracks develop. That appeared to be part of the Mounties' selection process rationale. From dawn to dark, the candidates were pushed and prodded to do more. They were asked to run, sprint, do push-ups, climb ropes, carry classmates on their backs, then sprint some more. They were harassed and harangued. Exhausted, they were pushed through obstacle courses, classroom lectures, and psychological situations where they were instructed to observe a scene, then subjected to more intense exercise, and later asked to recall in detail the specifics of what they had seen hours before. After grueling workouts, they were told to dress for dinner, then asked to be in full combat gear minutes later. Day after day, they were pushed, hassled, embarrassed and told they were inadequate and had to do better.

People broke down. Most didn't make it. Physically, they blew out knees and backs. Some quit mentally. A few survived. Cam certainly felt the pressure early. On Day 2, hurting and tired, he noticed himself becoming negative and self-critical. He started to think, "I'm not good enough ... I'm not going to make it." When he saw what was happening, Cam remembered to tune into his breathing and to remind himself "the waves keep rolling" ... and "that force is with me." As he tuned into the rhythm and continuity of his breath, Cam felt a surge of energy and the sense that he could go on. At that moment, he began to enjoy the challenge.

A third key to performing under pressure is **continuity.** This is the ability to tune in and experience a constant, continuous flow of energy.

~ One way to experience more continuity is to tune into the continuous wave after wave of your breath.

~ Just as the ocean waves can wear anything down,
   crush rock into sand,
   wash anything away,
   you can wash away tension,
   tiredness,
   dis-ease,
   and negativity
   simply by tuning into wave after wave of your breath.

~ Wave after wave,
   breath after breath,
   breathe in positive energy.

~ Release used, negative energy.

~ Experience wave after wave of your breath.

~ Experience a continuous flowing in ... and out.

~ The waves never stop.

~ Experience it for yourself.

~ First, make yourself comfortable.

~ Then, decide what you want to diminish.

~ Is it tension, fatigue, negativity?

~ Now, take twenty breaths.

~ As you do, connect your inbreath to your outbreath ...
  connect your outbreath to your inbreath.

~ Experience your breath as a continuous flow of energy in ... and
  out.

~ On the inbreath, feel yourself drawing in positive energy.

~ On the outbreath, feel yourself releasing tension, fatigue or
  negativity.

~ Wherever you are,
  whatever you're doing,
  tune into your breathing.

~ It can be a source of tremendous strength.

~ That force is with you.

~ As you experience twenty connected breaths, combine the
  feeling of continuity with these thoughts: "The waves never
  stop." "The force is with me."

As a cornerbacker for the Los Angeles Rams, Leroy Irvin saw himself as "a man on an island." "I'm on my own out there," he explained. "Everybody can see me, but no one can help me." His job involved the high-pressure, high-profile task of covering some of pro football's fastest and best receivers. A mistake, a lapse, a slip could mean a touchdown, or even the game for the opponent. To my mind, his was one of the toughest and most demanding jobs in all of pro sport.

He asked me for something that might give him an edge and keep him loose. He said he wanted something that would help him deal effectively with pressure, play after play.

Techniques have to be simple to be useful and effective under pressure. We developed a program and reinforced it with audio tapes. It was simple—in essence, experiencing the continuity of breath. Between plays, no matter what the score, or how much time was left in the game, no matter who he was covering or what had happened on the last play, Leroy would tune into his breathing. He would specifically focus on the continuity and power of the waves. Between every play, Leroy would remind himself to draw on the power of the waves. His experience was that play after play, breath after breath, the power was there for him. And the thought that he combined with his breathing was, "I'm in charge."

Leroy's ability to focus on his breathing between plays enabled him to reorganize and recharge after an all-out sprint down-field or a bone-jarring tackle. It gave him more consistency. It reduced the interference and stress. It allowed him to play his game. The two years we worked together, Leroy was a defensive standout and an NFL All-Pro. In a press interview, he described his response to our work. "My major problem throughout my career (seven seasons) has been consistency, and Saul got me into my inner self. He developed the wave for me. Got me into watching waves time and again. You know, they're so constant and consistent." And so was his play.

It's an age-old prescription. In Japan about 125 years ago, there lived a well-known wrestler named Onami (which means "great waves").* Onami was very strong and knew the art of wrestling. In his private matches, it was said that he defeated his teacher. However, in public, he was so shy and uneasy that even his own students threw him.

Onami felt that he should go to a Zen master for help. It just so happened that a wandering teacher was stopping at a little temple nearby, so Onami went to see him and told him of his trouble.

"Your name means great waves," said his teacher. "Stay in the temple tonight and imagine you are those waves. You're no longer a wrestler who's afraid. You are like huge waves sweeping away everything before them, swallowing up everything in their path. Do this and you will be the greatest wrestler in the land."

The teacher went to bed. Onami sat in meditation trying to imagine himself as waves. He thought of many things. Gradually his mind turned more and more to the feeling of waves. As the night advanced, the waves became larger and larger. They swept away everything in the temple. Even the Buddha in the shrine was inundated. Before dawn, the temple was nothing but the ebb and flow of an immense sea.

In the morning, the teacher found Onami meditating. There was a faint smile on his face. He patted the wrestler's shoulder. "Now

---

*Adapted from Reps, Paul. *Zen Flesh, Zen Bones*. Rutland, VT: Charles E. Tuttle Publishers, 1957.

nothing can disturb you," he said. "You are these waves. You will sweep away everything before you."

The same day, Onami entered the wrestling contests and won. After that, no one in Japan was able to defeat him.

~ Another way you can experience the power and continuity of
  the breath is to think of your breathing as being like a wheel.
~ As you breathe in, the wheel turns up ...
  as you breathe out, it turns down.

~ Experience your breath as an endlessly turning wheel.
~ As it turns, it generates energy.
~ As it turns, you generate energy.

~ To experience the continuity of the breath,
  take twenty breaths.
~ As you do, connect your inbreath to your outbreath ...
  connect your outbreath to your inbreath.
~ Turn the wheel.
~ Generate energy.
~ Transform stress.
~ Empower yourself.

~ Relax, breathe and think,
  the waves never stop,
  the wheel keeps turning.

In 1984 and 1988, I worked with many athletes in preparation for the Olympic Games in Los Angeles and Seoul. One process I used to give them more power and endurance was the idea of their breathing as turning a wheel.

One of the most limiting emotions a world-class athlete experiences is *fear*. It can take the form of a fear of failure, a fear of embarrassment, fear of the unknown, a fear of success or a fear of letting others down. A sense of great difficulty can also be limiting. By that, I mean thinking, "It's hard," "I don't know if I can ..." magnifies difficulty and alters performance.

It's the same for performers in most other fields. Whenever my clients experience limiting thoughts or feelings, I encourage them to tune into their breathing and *use the emotion* generated by the anxiety, adversity and discomfort they're feeling *to turn the wheel*. By coming back into their breathing whenever they feel fear and pressure and connecting the inbreath to the outbreath, they are better able to change adversity into power and to be more in charge.

Whenever you experience a negative thought or find yourself in a difficult or potentially embarrassing situation, transform the tendency to tense up and contract by simply going back to your breathing, *turning the wheel*, generating more energy and moving forward.

Chris was part of a four-man Canadian cycling team trying to make qualifying time for the 1988 Olympic Games in Seoul. Their task was to ride 100 kilometers in 2 hours, 5 minutes and 30 seconds. It was a challenge. The previous Canadian record in this event was 2 hours, 6 minutes and 40 seconds. To qualify, they had to cycle 1 minute and 10 seconds faster than any Canadian team had before.

Part of their psychological training addressed dealing effectively with the considerable tension and pain produced by that grueling event. I had repeatedly explained to each rider that it's much easier to be aggressive than to "hold on." "Holding on" changes nothing. It just means they had to ride their races at high speed while being tense and strained. Along with the thought of being aggressive, I showed each rider how when they felt pain and stress to focus on their breathing and turn the wheel.

In the qualifying race, the team went out very fast. After 20 kilometers, Chris said he started to feel pain and began to think, "just hold on." When he realized what he was thinking, he reminded himself, "it's easier to be aggressive than to hold on," and he went deeper into his breathing and picked up the pace. He rode a great race. The whole team did. They took 15 *minutes* off the previous Canadian record. Their time of 1: 15: 10 was an unofficial world record. It represents an amazing 13% performance jump … unheard of at world-class level. And one simple tool that helped Chris and his teammates make it all possible was their ability to focus on "turning the wheel."

CHAPTER 6 TRAINING NOTES

Coaching Continuity

1. As part of your daily ten-minute breathing session, experience wave after wave of the breath.

2. **During week three:** At least two or three times a day, take twenty *"connected breaths."* As you do, experience yourself connecting the inbreath to the outbreath … the outbreath to the inbreath.
    To reinforce the concept of continuity, repeatedly think of your breathing both as being like waves in the ocean and turning a wheel.
    Determine which image of "connecting" the breath, the waves or the wheel is more energizing or more tranquilizing for you. Then use that thought to give you a greater sense of ease and power throughout the day.

3. Some thoughts to combine with the feeling of energy, continuity and flow, include:

    "The breath is like an endlessly turning wheel."
    "The wheel (breath) keeps turning."

    "The waves never stop."
    "They can wash anything (tension, tiredness) away."

chapter seven

POWER POINTS

Many people allow pressure to push them out of the moment and into worrying and wondering about things that don't give them power.

One young pitcher I worked with pitched well in his first season in the big leagues. Then he seemed to lose his effectiveness. According to his account of what happened, it wasn't his fault. He was mismanaged. First, the coaching staff overused him and his arm got tired. When he was "down," they tried to stimulate him "up" by yelling at him. They ignored him. And lastly, they buried him in the bull pen without giving him any sense of his role or when he'd be used. The whole scenario eroded his confidence.

When I met him, he was angry, confused and not at all "in command." His focus was on the past, on *their* mistakes, *their* lack of understanding and *their* poor communication. He was worried about how much his pitching style had changed. And he was uncertain about the future and how he'd do his next time out.

I explained to him that the power is in the present and that in order to excel he had best focus his mind on what *he* could do *now*, and not what *they* had done in the *past*. I suggested that he focus on the positive and on the present, on the feelings he wanted to have on the mound, on the target he was throwing to and on the thought that he could do the job. He agreed, but then I'd see him slip into a cloud of negativity and become caught up with some of the "should haves" of his past.

To help him, I began to work with his breathing. I taught him how to focus on a specific point in his breath, a "power point" where he could feel that he was in the present. As he learned to focus on that point, he was better able to move away from worry and feel closer to where he had to be to really excel. Let me clarify.

When people focus on *outcome* (on the result they hope to achieve and the consequences of "making" or "not making" it), they often tense up, worry and limit themselves. Instead, I encourage my clients to focus on the present and the *process* of getting where they want to go.

One of the best pieces of advice I could offer any performer is to be "in the moment." One of the most effective ways to get into the moment is to focus into the breath … and to focus into power points.

Power points are those points where *the breath changes direction*. To experience them, follow your inbreath all the way in. As you do, determine the point where the inbreath starts to go out. That's the *peak point*. The peak point is a focus for a greater feeling of release and balance.

Next, follow the outbreath all the way out. Notice the point where the outbreath changes direction and starts to come in. That's the *source point*. It's the start of the next wave. The source point is a focus for greater feelings of inspiration and recharge.

The peak point and the source point are the two points where the breath changes direction. They are *power points*. They can also be focal points.

~ Experience twenty breaths.

~ For the first ten, focus on the peak point.

~ For the next, focus on the source point.

~ After you've repeated the process several times,
  determine which of the two is more accessible,
  more comfortable
  and more empowering.

~ Select one point as your focal point.

~ Use that power point.

~ Choose whichever works for you.

WHAT, ME WORRY?

For centuries, people have been looking for ways to calm themselves. A powerful and age-old technique to stop worrying is simply to relax and focus on a "centering" stimulus. As other thoughts come to mind, notice them ...then let them go; let them go ...
and bring the attention back to the focal point.

There's no more powerful, more personal, more dynamic or more effective stimulus than your breathing. Remember, anxieties and worries live in the past ("I should have ... or shouldn't have done that"). They live in the future ("what will happen if I do or don't ..."). And they live in our heads.

On the other hand, **the power is in the present**. To move out of worry and move more into the present, tune into the point where your breath changes direction. It's the point where you'll feel and perform at your best.

I was doing a *Sportstalk* radio show in Vancouver, British Columbia, when a caller phoned to say, "What I do is very similar to some of the sports you've been talking about. It requires a great deal of coordination, the ability to make hundreds of subtle movements, a tremendous amount of teamwork and being in very good shape. I'm a violinist for the Vancouver Symphony Orchestra.

He went on to explain that he was experiencing a dilemma. He had been a regular member of the VSO for years, playing up to 200 performances a season. With an impending dissolution of the orchestra, he was now faced with the extraordinarily high-pressure task of auditioning around North America. What he found at these auditions were ninety or more candidates competing for one job. The pressure was intense. He described how some of the musicians were using whatever techniques they thought might work to give them a competitive edge ... including "beta blockers."* He was worried and wanted to know what I might recommend for him.

What makes an audition (or any kind of employment interview) intense and sometimes problematic is that there is so much empha-

---

*"Beta blockers" are drugs that have principally been used in the treatment of high-blood pressure and heart disorders. They're increasingly being taken for their tranquilizing effect. They operate by blocking a major chemical reaction of the nervous system. Like most drugs, they have adverse side-effects. Most commonly, beta blockers upset the respiratory system, the nervous system and heart function. I advise my clients not to use them. Relying on drugs rather than oneself to create a psychological performance edge is almost always a *limiting* experience.

sis almost entirely on "outcome," that is, something in the future, as opposed to "process," the experience of playing and expressing expertise, and being in the moment. One of the best ways I know to shift someone from outcome into process is by guiding them into their breathing. As they tune into their breathing, specifically into the power point where the inbreath becomes an outbreath, they move back into the moment.

I recommended that the violinist tune into his breathing and give himself time for his inbreath to come all the way in. Then I directed him to the point where his breath changed direction. I encouraged him to sit quietly and do a minimum of ten minutes of power point breathing every day for a week. The following week, I suggested he do at least five minutes of rhythmic power point breathing while holding his violin. Then, I encouraged him to begin to play the instrument while maintaining this enhanced breathing awareness.

As this violinist's breathing consciousness developed, I encouraged him to return his focus to the elements and mechanics of playing well. Things like focusing on the feeling of cradling the violin, the feeling of the bow on the strings, the sensation of bowing and fingering with sensitivity and freedom. One aspect of reducing pressure and excelling involves releasing worries and uncertainties of the future and concerns for mistakes of the past ... and instead functioning in the present.

After the telephone call, the talk show host mused, "We've had calls about everything from baseball to sailing, from football to golf. But that's the first time in the five-year history of *Sportstalk* that someone had actually called to enquire about playing the violin."

I wasn't surprised by the call. I've worked with a number of musicians, singers and actors. Many of the same aspects of excelling under pressure apply in both theaters of performance. One of them is being in the moment ... and to maintain this under pressure, breathing is key.

~ Experience the simplicity and impact of this last key for yourself.
~ Take twenty breaths.
~ Follow each inbreath in to the peak, the power point ... then release.
~ Experience the point where each breath changes direction.
~ As thoughts, worries, distractions come to mind, notice them, release them ... and come back into your breathing.
~ Follow your next inbreath to the peak.
~ Gradually, you'll increase your ability to stay with this breath and this moment ... and worries, distractions and doubt will disappear.

THERE'S POWER IN SIMPLICITY

I was demonstrating breathing "like the waves" to a golfer who wanted something that would give him a little more emotional control under pressure. He told me he had tried some "breathing exercises" in the past, but they were complicated and caused him to think too much about his breathing, so he never really got into it.

He experienced breathing like the waves for a few moments.

"It feels good," he said, "but it's so simple. After I breathe in, shouldn't I do something like hold my breath for a few seconds?"

I asked him to think of the ocean waves and to imagine waves of power rolling in, wave after wave. Then I asked, "Does the ocean stop and hold after each wave?"

There's power in simplicity. In my experience, the breathing process described in this section is more simple, more natural and more practical than most of the standard breathing techniques taught in stress management classes, yoga, meditation and the martial arts. There's no holding, no counting, no forcing and no controlling. Breathing simply involves three keys: rhythm, inspiration and continuity ... and focusing on the point where the breath changes direction.

I've coached people in using their breathing for everything from winning ball games and increasing sales to having babies ... and it works.

WAVES OF POWER: A REVIEW

Breathing is basic to consistent high-level performance. In most of the performance training and seminars I do, I spend time reviewing the breathing keys. I find that just talking about breathing brings more ease.

At an interlude in a performance seminar, I was approached by a man who introduced himself as a banker. "I've always thought that qualities like patience, focus and controlled aggression are essential to being a good negotiator," he said. "I've read many books and attended innumerable seminars and conferences on the subject, and I'm clear that none of that input is any more relevant or more helpful than the breathing techniques you just described. They're basic."

I thanked him. Then I reminded him that there was one more essential to making the breathing keys work. "It's important to remember to use them throughout the day, especially when you're under pressure."

You can breathe with more ease and power in everything you do. Experience the breathing keys to performing under pressure for yourself. Observe the impact of your breathing on how you think, feel and perform.

RHYTHM   ~ Experience the rhythm of your breath.
~ Give yourself time for the inbreath to become an outbreath.
~ The waves never rush.
~ You deserve your time.

INSPIRATION ~ You have a personal connection to unlimited energy.
~ Focus on the inbreath, on drawing in energy.
~ Inspire yourself in everything you do.

CONTINUITY   ~ Connect the inbreath to the outbreath ... the
               outbreath to the inbreath ...
             ~ The breath is like an endlessly turning wheel.
             ~ It's wave after wave.
             ~ The waves never stop.

FOCUS ON A   ~ For greatest focus and impact, be in the moment.
POWER POINT ~ Tune into the point where the breath changes
               direction.
             ~ The power is in the moment.
             ~ The power is with the breath.

section three

RELEASE

———

One of the most common performance problems that people have is that they're just too tight in trying to excel, succeed and win, they often push, effort and "squeeze" too much. In doing this, they reduce their effectiveness and pleasure. In many cases, the tension they create causes them to lock in the very uncertainty and fear that they want to eliminate.

Two of the best reasons I can think of for learning how to release tension are: 1. it feels pleasurable, and 2. it enhances performance. For many of my clients, an effective way to help them develop more ease and greater mind-body control is to have them begin by working with something real, something they're in touch with and something they can appreciate ... learning to relax their bodies.

The word "relax" comes from the root word "laxus," which means to be loose. To relax, then, means to regain a natural feeling of looseness. The relaxation techniques I describe in this section are:

1. the "release reflex,"
2. "clearing the screen,"
3. scanning, and
4. streaming.

These are all basic to performance and wellbeing. They release blocks and inhibitions. They allow more energy to flow. And they promote greater awareness and control.

chapter eight

THE RELEASE REFLEX

For centuries in the Orient, all phenomena, including health and performance, were viewed in terms of two equal and opposite forces which were called *yin* and *yang*.

Yin is an expansive, dispersing force. Yang is a contractive, concentrating one. In these terms, most of the performance problems I deal with have strong yang features. That's because under pressure ... and in their intense desire to excel, many performers tense up and contract.

To help them move toward balance and excellence, I teach them to *release*.

Allow yourself to imagine what it would feel like to be a professional golfer about to attempt a ten-foot putt late in a close match with thousands of dollars riding on its outcome.

Imagine being a salesperson about to call on one of your biggest accounts, knowing that they're contemplating a change.

Imagine being a concert musician, a soloist about to perform in front of a thousand people ... and not feeling confident.

Imagine having to make a major marketing (or loan) decision now, in a prevailing context of uncertainty.

Imagine being an actor or a student about to read or interview for an important career opportunity.

In each case, you may experience a natural "defensive" tendency to tighten up, to contract, to feel "pressured," and in so doing, to limit yourself.

The *release reflex* is a simple, powerful, conscious response that effectively releases contraction and allows you to be at your best.

THE CONTRACTIVE REFLEX

Whenever a person perceives a dangerous or threatening stimulus, there's a natural, reflexive reaction to contract. This contractive reflex usually involves a tightening of the neck and shoulder muscles, followed instantly by a tensing of muscles throughout the body. The exact pattern is specific to each one of us. It's a defensive posture that prepares us for fight or flight, and it's part of our basic survival instinct.

Many things can trigger this contractive reflex. They range from some very real external physical stimulus to some vague personal perception of danger.

For human beings, criticism, insult, fear of failure and embarrassment can all trigger the contractive reflex. And it's not just what others say to us that can cause us to tighten up. The mind doesn't distinguish the source of the threat. Our own fear, negative thinking and self-talk can also produce the contraction. Indeed, for many of my clients, the most frequent source of tension, contraction and dis-ease is what they say to themselves:

"I don't think I can."

"I'm not so sure ... " (of myself).

"I should be able to ... "

"Maybe I won't."

"What if I don't?"

"I can't."

"Who cares?"

"Oh, no ... not again."

"Damn. What's wrong with me?"

"I've got to do it ... " (to feel good about myself)

"What'll they think?"

"I'm inadequate ... "

The bottom line of this is that "I'm not okay."

Mind and body are one. Each thought we have is expressed in our physical bodies and in our breathing. Thoughts of confidence and competence generally promote inspiration, expansion and feelings of ease and power. Thoughts of fear, worry and negativity create contraction, tension, limitation and feelings of dis-ease.

What's also important to realize is that the contractive reflex (which is part of our defensive wiring) can, when we tense up, actually "lock in" some of the negative and limiting thoughts that triggered it. These are the very thoughts we wish to avoid. The result of locking in the negative or fearful thought is usually more pressure and more dis-ease.

An effective antidote to this pressure circle is to develop your release reflex and learn how to use tension as a stimulus to **release and breathe**.

THE RELEASE REFLEX

The principle of change and the release reflex is remarkably simple. Whenever you feel tension or contraction, release it … and take a breath.

Tension   Release and Breathe

Don't hold tension, don't carry it around. Release it … and breathe.

Release and Breathe

Don't fight tension or worry about outcome … instead, use your situation as a stimulus to trigger release.

Release and Breathe

Just as we all have a tension contraction reflex, an automatic survival response, you can also develop a *release reflex*, an almost automatic way to *use tension to trigger release.*

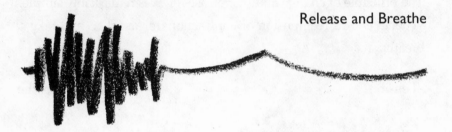

Release and Breathe

The ability to **release under pressure** is an integral part of the response repertoire of most consistent high-level performers.

As he steps up to putt, the golfer experiences some tension in his hands and shoulders. He hears himself thinking, "Don't miss this one." Then he stops. He shifts from outcome to process. He releases tension in his shoulders. He takes a breath. He refocuses on a good feeling in his hands. He readjusts his grip. He thinks, "I have great touch." He images the ball rolling into the cup. Then he plays the shot.

The saleswoman reluctantly picks up the phone. She knows the buyer she's about to call was really annoyed with their last order, which was very late. Suddenly she feels tired. She notices an uncomfortable feeling in her solar plexus. She hears herself think, "The damn production unit. It won't be my fault if he doesn't write any business."

Then she sees the process and stops. She releases some of the tension. She takes a few breaths focusing on the inbreath ... on the present. The negativity diminishes. She refocuses. She thinks, "I'm effective, I sell a fine product. We've got a good program. And, I enjoy a challenge. ... " She smiles, then dials the buyer's number.

When you feel tension   release it ...   breathe ...   and refocus.

Use tension to trigger   your release reflex.

Stanley was a virtuoso concerto violinist. In his forty-year career, he had played internationally with some of the world's finest orchestras. In the last few years, he developed a specific performance problem, something he considered a "memory problem." In concert, he would sometimes forget the music and "go blank." After this occurred on a couple of occasions, he began to worry and wonder when it would happen next.

The phenomenon of "going blank" is not limited to musicians. I've seen it affect actors, students, public speakers ... even quarterbacks. In Stanley's case, the anxiety and embarrassment of "blanking out" destroyed the ease and joy he experienced playing in concert. It diminished the quality of his play. It reduced the number of engagements he sought. And it contributed to him thinking less well of himself.

After working with Stanley and watching him play a number of times, it was clear to me that "the problem" wasn't his memory at all. It was his struggle in dealing with the pressure of performing in concert. Stanley was a perfectionist. He had a highly developed critical sense and was driven to "do it right." He was also a very sensitive performer who created a considerable amount of tension playing in front of a large, and what he perceived to be critical, audience. The combination of his desire to be perfect, his sensitivity and his perception of the audience as sitting in judgment caused him to become tense and overaroused.

In the course of a violin concerto with thousands of minute moves and difficult high-speed runs, it's inevitable that any performer will make a few minor slips. In his hypercritical state with his intense desire to be perfect, Stanley overreacted to these minor glitches. Instead of just flowing on when they occurred, they would trigger his contractive reflex. He would tighten up, hold his breath, slip out of the flow of the music, get lost, panic and "go blank."

To help Stanley to perform with more impact and joy, I worked with him to develop his release reflex and his ability to control the "switch" on his mental TV. The idea was that any time Stanley would notice a slip and feel himself start to tense up and contract ... he would release, breathe and flow on with the music. To do that, we spent a dozen hours working with his ability to release and breathe. In addition, I encouraged Stanley to practice making errors, to release and to keep right on playing through them. The idea was to reorient his thinking from "trying to play perfectly" and anticipating an error to focusing on and expecting to play beautifully. Which he did.

One of the more unusual techniques that Stanley and I used to strengthen his release reflex is worthwhile repeating.

At the time I consulted with Stanley, I was living in a lovely mountain valley in southern California. My house was situated next to a cold mountain stream and about 350 yards from a natural hot spring. I spent a few hours talking with Stanley, listening to and observing him play and showing him the breathing keys. Then, I accompanied him to the hot mineral spring. As Stanley relaxed in the warm water, I reminded him to breathe easily and "release." After a few minutes of relaxing (releasing and breathing), I instructed Stanley to submerge himself in the icy cold mountain stream.

The shock of the cold stream fired his contractive reflex, took his breath away. It provided Stanley with an excellent opportunity to practice releasing and breathing. With a little practice of hot springs ... cold stream, Stanley was able to release and breathe in the cold water. We repeated the cycle several times each session. Not only was it a powerful training stimulus, it was thoroughly invigorating.* To further reinforce that effect at home, I recommended that Stanley practice releasing and breathing while shifting from hot to cold several times in the shower each morning.

As Stanley become more and more proficient at exercising his "release reflex," I encouraged him to integrate his ability into his hours of musical practice ... particularly at those moments when he noticed himself tensing up and holding.

---

*While I consider the above excellent therapy and good fun (something I did daily), medical and legal considerations, plus good sense, prompt me to limit recommending the experience only to those people in good health and free from heart or circulatory problems.

chapter nine

TENSION RELEASE
AND SCANNING

Did you ever say "relax" to someone who is tense or uptight? If people don't know how to do it, the advice rarely helps.

Rob was an excellent young golfer. He possessed some of the best natural ability on the college golf circuit. He could hit the ball long and he had excellent touch around the greens. His only problem was that he didn't perform well under pressure. Rob was at his best playing by himself or when the competition was so low key that his performance didn't really seem to matter. Of course, that wasn't good enough. As we said earlier, success in a competitive forum demands increasingly more challenging competition and the ability to deal with more and more pressure. To really compete and excel, Rob had to be effective in close matches and in high-pressure situations.

Rob struggled in tournaments. He would get tense and lose effectiveness as the pressure built up. Both his long and short game were affected. It was pretty clear that the thing to do was to help him become more relaxed under pressure. The question was, how?

Talking to Rob and observing him play, I knew that what he was thinking and saying to himself was causing him to tense up. And that this tightening up contributed to more negative self-talk. It was a vicious circle. I chose not to address the self-talk directly, at least not at first. Rob was a sensitive introvert who was easily distracted and upset. I thought that teaching him the basics of tension release would help him shift his focus from all the things out there that he couldn't control to something he was familiar with and something he could control … his muscles.

As Rob began to exercise more control over his body, he experienced more consistency and ease. We began working on what Rob was thinking and on high-performance imagery. To further insulate Rob from the stress of competition, we had him practice relaxing and playing with golf partners who were instructed to be provocative and irritating. (That's not too difficult to arrange on a university golf team!)

As I've said before, sport is a metaphor. In Rob's case, the problem he had dealing with pressure on the golf course paralleled the difficulties he experienced with exam pressure and in expressing himself in groups. In consulting with Rob, we focused exclusively on his ability to relax as it related to golf. What's interesting is that as Rob developed the habit of releasing and breathing on the golf course his confidence seemed to grow and his ability to express himself in all performance areas improved.

TENSION RELEASE

One of the easiest and most effective ways to help my clients is to show them the breathing keys and then have them do a little tension release. By this, I mean having them practice tensing and then releasing specific parts of their bodies.

Tension release is a popular treatment process. The two main reasons I use it, are: 1. creating tension exaggerates the feeling of release, and that's the feeling we want to highlight; and 2. tensing and releasing specific muscle groups is a focusing exercise, one that will help to develop more control and enhance your ability to "change channels."

Tension release is a simple, effective way to start developing "control of the switch."

To begin, guide attention to your hands.

The hands are an area over which we have awareness and control. As such, they're an ideal place to being practicing your mastery over physical tension. The same principle of release, breathe and refocus that was described in Chapter 8 applies to the whole body and is most easily illustrated here with your hands.

Create some tension in your hands by making fists.

Squeeze the fists. Feel the tension in the center core of the fist and between the fingers. Hold it four to five seconds.

Release … let it go.

After you release, take a breath.

It's that feeling of release and breathe that I recommend you experience and be able to recall.

Create tension ...   hold it ...   release ...   breathe ...   refocus.

THE RELEASE PRINCIPLE
INVOLVES USING TENSION AND PRESSURE
TO TRIGGER RELEASE

Remember, what we're practicing here isn't just about relaxing the hands. It's about developing your awareness and your ability to release tension. And it's about being in charge of your reactions and "changing channels."

Instead of feeling stress and under the effect of what's happening around you, use the situation to release and refocus.

~ Once again, make fists.
~ Feel the tension.
~ Exaggerate that feeling by turning in the wrists.
~ Hold this (four to five seconds).
~ Then, release ... and breathe.
~ That's the feeling you want to experience and to be able to recreate.

Next, move your attention to your neck and shoulders.

The neck and shoulder area is the *primary* tension-holding area in the body. It's the number one place where people tighten up and pull back under pressure.

~ Raise your shoulders up two to three inches.
~ Feel the tension that is created in the neck and around the collarbones.
~ Hold this (four to five seconds).

~ Release ... and breathe.
~ Experience the feeling of letting go.
~ As you do, allow the head to come out, the spinal cord to lengthen and the neck to be full.
~ It's that feeling you want to recall and recreate.

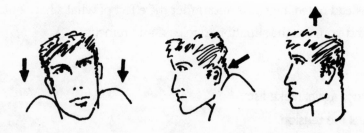

~ One way to stimulate your defensive contraction reflex is to raise your shoulders just half an inch.
~ Experience the considerable amount of pressure created by such a subtle move.
~ Hold this (four to five seconds).
~ Release and breathe.

By voluntarily creating this response, and then releasing it and breathing, you can develop greater awareness and control of that mechanism and a greater sense of freedom and ease.

Since 1970, I've spent several years in Europe and North America studying the Alexander Technique. This technique (named after its founder) is a "hands-on" process that teaches people to become more aware of how they use themselves. It enables them to perform with more ease and more effectiveness.

What I enjoy about the Alexander Technique is that it adds a direction to the idea of release. The technique has two basic principles. The first is *release*. In our terms, that simply means when you experience tension, release it (take a breath) and refocus. The second involves the primacy of the head-torso relationship. By that, I mean organization in the body proceeds from the top downwards; the head leads and the body follows. In practical terms it means release the contractive response in the head-neck area and *allow the head to move forward and up*. The rest of the body will follow.

What seems to happen is that in overefforting and "trying" people tighten up, contract and pull themselves down (A). Refocusing involves letting go of this contraction and directing or guiding the head to move forward and up, to *ease up* (B). Easing up in this manner enhances the response quality throughout the body. What I've observed is that when people contract and pull down they often "slump." And when they slump they usually pull down and contract. One way out of a slump is to release ... breathe ... and think of easing your head forward and up.

A. Pulling down   **B.** Easing up

The Alexander Technique is essentially an experiential way to facilitate both easing up and performance, any kind of performance. In general, musicians, actors and dancers have been more responsive to it than athletes and the business community. This is partly due to the preoccupation with feeling and response in the arts, and an unwillingness that athletes and business people often have to let go of their "at any price" attitude.

A basic way to support yourself and experience less stress is to release, breathe and allow your head to ease up. Your body will follow.

Now guide your attention to your jaws.

The jaws and teeth are a part of our most primitive self-defense mechanism. Tension, anger, frustration and aggression are all stored and expressed in the jaws. It's an important area to work on to overcome some of our basic responses to pressure.

~ Tighten your jaws and clench your teeth.
~ To exaggerate tension in and around the mouth, part your lips to expose your clenched teeth.
~ Feel the tension that is created in your mouth, cheeks and jaws.
~ Hold this (four to five seconds).

~ Now let it go.
~ Release ... and breathe.
~ It's that feeling of letting go you want to experience and recreate.
~ A genuine smile is a great release.
~ When people smile, they reflexively release the muscles in their face and jaw ... plus a good deal more inside.

~ A fake smile is another story.
~ It's an expression of fear and dis-ease.
~ A fake smile involves tensing many of the same muscles we contracted in tightening the jaw.
~ Check this yourself.

~ Create a fake smile.

~ Hold it.

~ Feel the mask of tension you are creating in your face.

~ Notice you're also holding your breath.

~ Now release ... and breathe.

~ The feeling of release is what you should experience and recreate.

~ Fake smiles are epidemic.

~ You can see them everywhere.

~ Whenever you spot one, use it
  as a stimulus or reminder for you to release and breathe.

~ Remember, you're the boss.

~ And you control the switch.

Now, guide attention to your chest and abdomen. Two of the main energy centers of the body are located in the upper chest and lower abdomen.

~ Place one hand on your upper chest and one on your lower
  abdomen.

~ Relax and breathe.

~ Your hands are like biofeedback sensors.

~ They're there to remind you to allow your chest and abdomen
  to be free to expand and contract with each breath you take.

~ With each wave of your breath, feel your chest and abdomen
   rise and fall ... freely and rhythmically.

~ Allow yourself to become a little more relaxed with each breath
   you take.

~ Relax and breathe.

~ Breathing is power. Tension cuts down breathing. Less breathing
   means less power ... and less ease.

~ Experiment for yourself.

~ Keeping your hands on your chest and abdomen,
   tighten your abdominal muscles
   (as you might to protect yourself from a poke in the stomach).

~ Hold this.

~ Notice, of course, *you've stopped breathing*.

~ Now release and breathe.

~ Go back a step.

~ Keeping your hands on your chest and abdomen,
   raise your shoulders half an inch.

~ Hold this.

~ Notice, again, you've stopped or cut down your breathing.

~ Release and breathe.

~ These exercises needn't be repeated. We do them to
   demonstrate that tension and contraction limit breathing.
   And breathing is power and ease.

~ Release and breathe.

To "choke" means to tighten up under pressure, to cut down breathing and to perform poorly. It's one of those popular terms that people apply to almost any performance situation.

When Carole swam butterfly, she loved to swim from the lead. When she sensed the competition closing in on her, she would tighten up (especially in the shoulders). In so doing, she would lose speed and power ... and fade. I was asked to help her develop an alternative to contracting (and "choking") under pressure.

What we worked on was using tensing (in this case, her perception of people catching up to her) as a stimulus to release (tension) ... breathe (draw in energy) ... and accelerate. Instead of Carole sensing the competition closing in and tightening up, we wanted her response to that stimulus to be, breathe in energy and think "power, speed, ease" or think "free shoulders," "stretch and pull," or "shark" (as in, "I slice through the water like a shark").

To do this, we worked together half a dozen times three weeks prior to an important national meet. It was sufficient time and training for Carole to learn how to put the "release reflex" to work under pressure. In her first (qualifying) heat at the Canadian National Championships, she took the lead, lost it, and then, instead of tensing and "choking," Carole released, breathed deeper, refocused ... and came roaring back to win.

"Choking" can be eliminated. Being able to reproduce a contractive response and then release it gives us greater control of that response. It increases the probability that we can and will release and refocus under pressure.

If you are in the habit of tensing a certain part of your body in response to a specific stimulus or challenge, practice tension release.

Like Carole, you can learn to use any high-pressure stimulus as a reminder to release, breathe and refocus.

A basic rule of relaxation is that:

TENSION CAN LEAD TO MORE TENSION
UNLESS YOU USE IT

If you feel yourself being tense or tensing up, release ... breathe ... refocus. If you experience others as tense, use their tension to remind you to release and breathe.

I often see people with a lot of tension in their bodies. I don't look for it. I prefer to see ease ... and smiles. However, when I observe their dis-ease I use it to remind myself to release my own tension and breathe.

Use tension as a stimulus to create ease. Remember, if you don't use it, it may use you.

~ Now guide your attention to your sexual organs.

~ This is another primary tension-holding area.

~ There's a muscle plexus or sphincter in the genital area that we sometimes tighten and squeeze under pressure, when we hold back in sex, and in going to the toilet.

~ Tighten that muscle plexus.

~ Hold this (four to five seconds).

~ Notice you've probably cut down your breathing.

~ Now release ... and breathe.

~ That's the feeling you want to recall.

~ You can tense or release any part of your body.*
~ You can release tension in your body or your mind.
~ You control the switch.

A Question I'm Frequently Asked

While waiting for a table in a very popular Los Angeles restaurant, I was introduced to the owner by my companion. My friend mentioned my work in professional sport and the restauranteur asked for some instant advice on improving his golf game. "When I play golf and I'm relaxed, I play great," he said. "But when it's important to me, like when I'm playing with friends and there's a few dollars on the hole, it becomes a matter of pride to me and I get tense, I rush and

---

*For men, another genital-release response involves relaxing the testicles. When men are stressed under pressure (threatened), there's a contractive reflex tendency to tighten up and withdraw the testicles. That is, to draw them up in the direction of into the body (though the actual contraction is minimal). In contrast, when men are feeling relaxed, at ease (safe), there's a subtle release of that mechanism which allows the testicles to descend more fully. In women, it's similar in some respects to nursing mothers relaxing, releasing and "letting down their milk."

Some people, like advanced yogis, have developed the ability to regulate many of the body's seemingly autonomic (automatic) functions, including withdrawing or lowering the testicles voluntarily. Obviously, it's a fairly developed response. While most men have the capacity, few have the control. For our purposes, the specific testicle release response is not highly significant in and of itself. However, it does reflect a capacity for greater awareness and control; one that I often encourage and train my clients to develop.

play terribly. What can you suggest that would help me to be more calm and play better?"

Two things came to my mind. First, I told him to breathe easy. To give himself time for the inbreath to come all the way in, and the outbreath to go all the way out. And, I showed him exactly what I meant. Second, I said "Relax your balls. Allow them to release and descend as you set up ... before every shot."

He looked at me strangely, and nodded.

I asked him, "What do you do in your work that causes you to be tense?"

"Are you kidding?" he exclaimed. "Do you know how many things can go wrong in a place like this? I'm tense here all the time."

"Okay," I replied, "whenever you notice you're tense or whenever you catch yourself thinking of something that could or did go wrong, remember to do what I told you to do before each golf shot. Take a breath. Give yourself time ... and then relax your testicles. Not only will it help you to be more at ease and deal with things here more effectively, the continuous practice will improve your golf game."

For many people, the habit of tensing the genitals in an attempt to be "in control" began in our toilet training days when we were two years old. Holding your breath or tensing a sphincter is an understandable and common defensive response to pressure, but it won't improve your play. Being able to exercise greater control of subtle, intimate responses will. It's a tip I've shared with PGA tour golfers and businessmen alike.

~ The last tension release exercise involves curling your toes.

~ Make fists with your feet.

~ Feel the tension in the soles of your feet and the toes.

~ Hold this (four to five seconds).

~ It's like a bird holding onto a perch. Performers with busy hands (for example, jugglers, batters) and those who are high-profile (actors on stage, speakers in front of an audience) often clench their feet as an expression of tension. In so doing, they limit the flow of energy up through the body and lose power.

~ Now release and breathe.

~ Think *"cat's feet."*

~ Feel yourself with power pads on the soles of your feet and toes.

~ It's a feeling that will give you more spring and balance.

~ And it's one to recall and recreate.

Creating "cat's feet" is a valuable performance aid. I've used it with athletes in over twenty different sports. But it's not limited to the athlete. The concept of "cat's feet" is for anyone who can appreciate better grounding and balance, and the power that comes from the sense of having a secure base.

Tension release is a popular relaxation technique. However, our approach to the technique differs from many of the other people who advocate it. For one thing, I *pair release with breathing* for a more powerful effect.

What's most significant, however, is that the tension release process we're describing is only a brief, *temporary* phase of the total performing under pressure experience. Remember, what's really important is not that you have the ability to tense or release six or seven different parts of the body, but rather that you develop greater awareness and mind-body control.

After you've practiced the tension release exercises about eight to ten times, it's no longer productive to make tension in order to create release. The exception is when one area (say the neck and shoulders) is feeling uncomfortably tight and you can't seem to relax it. Exaggerating the feeling of dis-ease, by raising up the shoulders ... then releasing and breathing, often releases the tension and creates a greater sense of ease. After this, you can simply "scan" over your body, tune in ... release ... breathe ... and refocus.

SCANNING

Scanning is a two- to three-second process
of tuning into your body,
picking up any unnecessary, undesirable tension,
releasing it ...
and taking a breath.
There's no forced tension.
It's just tuning in and releasing.

Over the years, I've consulted with a wide variety of clients. The list includes golfers, pitchers, linebackers, coaches, salespeople, stockbrokers, writers, actors, musicians, teachers, doctors and lawyers. Two things they all have in common are a desire to excel, and the opportunity while doing what they do to take a couple of seconds, scan the body and release unnecessary tension and refocus.

~ To begin the scanning process, release and breathe.
~ Tune into the three breathing keys.
~ Rhythm: give yourself time for the inbreath to become an outbreath.
~ Inspiration: focus on drawing in power.
~ Continuity: connect the inbreath to the outbreath, wave after wave.
~ Pick up the point where the breath changes direction.

~ Now guide attention to your hands.
~ Experience the feeling of release in the hands, arms and fingers.
~ Release ... breathe ... (draw in energy).

~ Tune into your neck and shoulders.
~ Recall the feeling of raising up the shoulders half an inch and then letting them go.
~ Release ... breathe ... (allow the head to move up and the spinal cord to lengthen).

~ Guide attention to your jaws.
~ Allow the muscles in the jaws, cheeks and around the mouth to release ... and breathe.

~ Allow your chest and abdomen to be free … to rise and fall with
  each breath.

~ Allow your genitals to relax.
~ Recall the feeling of letting go.
~ Release and breathe.
~ Allow the muscles in your feet to relax.
~ Think "cat's feet."
~ Release and breathe.

With practice, the entire scanning process takes just a few seconds.

~ For a three-second scan, release and breathe.
~ Allow your hands, shoulders, jaw, chest, abdomen,
  genitals and feet to release … and breathe.

You've probably seen it many times. In a baseball game in front of
thousands of spectators and a television audience of millions, a
pitcher will step off the mound, scan, release, take a breath, refocus,
step back on the mound and go back to work. Similarly, his adver-
sary in the baseball drama will step out of the batter's box, run
through his routine to release tension, breathe and step back up to
the plate.

Performance is the bottom line. Both performers know that when
they're loose and relaxed they'll perform better. Most players are
aware of the specific areas they tense up. Ideally, they take a second
or two to scan the body, cue these spots, release the interference,
breathe and refocus. That's what I recommend.

CHAPTER 9 TRAINING NOTES

Tension Release

1. **Week one**: Along with the breathing session, spend ten
    minutes a day tensing and *releasing* each of the six muscle
    groups described in Chapter Nine ... plus any other areas
    you may want to focus on.

    Remember, tension release is a temporary training phase.
    After you can discriminate differences between tension and
    release, it's no longer necessary to create tension in order to
    release.

2. As you tense and release, remind yourself:

    "I control the switch."
    "I can release tension in any part of my body."
    "I deserve to feel good."

Scanning

3. **Week two**: After a week of tension release, spend three
    minutes as part of your daily "breathing session" scanning
    and releasing.

4. At least two or three times a day for weeks two, three and
    four, take thirty seconds or a minute to scan ... release ... and
    breathe. Whether you're at home, at work or at play, develop
    the habit of being "at ease." Develop the habit of scanning
    and releasing.

5. Again, remind yourself:

   "I control the switch."
   "I'm the master of my reactions."
   "I deserve to feel good."

chapter ten

STREAMING

Streaming is about flow. On the physical level, it involves releasing tension and blocks in the body, breathing easily, drawing in energy, then guiding, directing and allowing this energy to flow through the body. Streaming is about experiencing more ease, and then channeling the flow of energy to any part of your body … or out into the world around you.

Streaming can be a *ten- to twenty-minute* process in which you sit or lie back, breathe easily, release tension and send energy throughout the body, or to some specific part of the body where you experience tension or dis-ease. The body is like a rechargeable battery. And streaming is a relaxing, recharging, regenerative process.

Streaming, like scanning, can also be a *five- to ten-second* process in which you release, breathe and send your energy out. It's an energizing, stress-reducing preparation exercise.

Downhill racers are an interesting breed. The good ones have the ability to be aggressive and stay loose at the same time. Gary Athans told me a story of skiing in Europe. He was racing down a slope in

Switzerland hitting speeds of sixty-five to seventy miles per hour when his binding popped loose and his ski flew off. "What did you do?" I asked. "I had a great time going," he replied matter of factly, "so, I tried to finish the race on one ski."

When I first met Gary, he was a member of the Canadian ski team. he was a very talented and motivated young man in outstanding physical condition. However, he was experiencing a great deal of leg fatigue on the long downhill courses, and this significantly interfered with his peformance. He had become so frustrated and depressed about his inability to compete that he had considered quitting. The medical team had checked him out, and he scored as one of the most well-conditioned athletes on the team. He was referred to me for consultation.

After talking with Gary and testing him, it seemed to me that he had two problems. One, he was pressing too hard. (Many of the performance problems I encounter involve overstriving, pushing, pressing or squeezing too much. Gary was no exception.) Two, his mind and body weren't synchronized. It was as though he was thinking at 120 m.p.h. and moving at fifty.

I began to teach Gary to relax. One of the best ways to teach balance and integration is to show people how to relax. We started with breathing and tension release. As Gary began to breathe more easily and let go of some of the tension, I suggested he do some streaming. He practiced drawing in energy and sending it out through the body … especially sending it down through his legs and feet.

Streaming is an active process. If there's a part of your body that's tense, tired or sore, don't avoid it. Instead, focus on this. Release tension in that spot, then stream energy to it … and through it.

With practice, Gary understood how to use the release principle and streaming to be looser, more at ease and "power-full." As he began to exercise more control of his body and to release, breathe and stream, his leg fatigue disappeared. His confidence grew. Ease and joy returned to his skiing. His endurance increased, and Gary gave up thoughts of an early retirement. He continued to race internationally for another five years.

STREAMING

Like most things, the best way to learn streaming is to do it.

~ To begin, make yourself comfortable ...
  and tune into your breathing.
~ Pick up the three keys: rhythm, inspiration and continuity.
~ Now scan the body and release any unnecessary tension.
~ As you move through the body, recall the feeling of letting go.
~ Allow your hands, arms and shoulders to release ... and breathe.
~ Allow your jaw and face to relax and breathe.
~ Allow your chest and abdomen to be free to expand and contract.
~ Let go of tension in the legs and feet ... and breathe.
~ With each breath, draw in energy ... then send it out through your body.
~ Send it out to *the five points*.

Points 1 and 2—The Hands

Breathe in energy. On the outbreath, send or allow energy to flow out through your chest, shoulders and arms, down through the palms of your hands into the fingers.

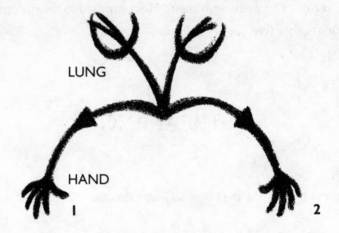

Points 3 and 4—The Legs and Feet

On the inbreath, draw in energy. On the outbreath, send or allow that energy to flow out and down through your pelvis, the legs and into the soles of your feet and toes.

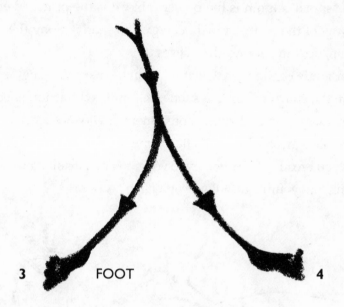

FOOT

3   4

Draw in energy. Stream it out ... through your pelvis, the legs and into the soles of your feet.

Point 5—The Spinal Column and Head

On the inbreath, draw in energy. On the outbreath, send or allow that energy to flow out. Allow it to flow along the spinal column, up through your neck, into the top of your head and your eyes.

The spinal column is the power cable. It is the principal energy pathway of the body. Draw in energy and send it along the spinal column, up into your head and eyes.

Tension is contraction. Creating a subtle, natural "lengthening" within the spinal column (a subtle, self-induced traction effect) releases the tension and stress stored there. It allows energy to flow. The result is greater ease and effectiveness.

As you breathe, draw energy to you. Stream it up along the spinal column into your head. Allow yourself to "ease up."

Remember, you have a personal connection to an unlimited supply of energy.

~ On the inbreath, draw in some of that energy.
~ On the outbreath, send it out, allow it to flow out simultaneously
   through the shoulders and arms into the palms of the hands and
   fingers ...
   through the pelvis and the legs, into the soles of the feet and
   toes ...
   through the spinal column, up into the eyes ...
   like a five-pointed star.

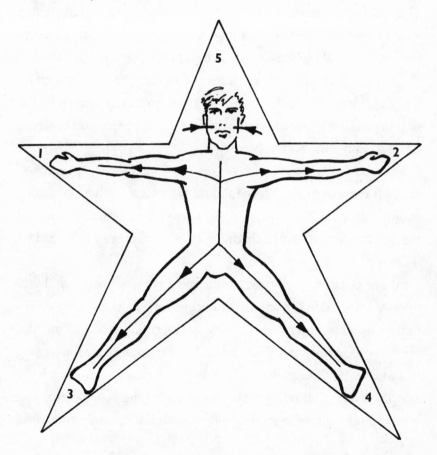

In the sensory cortex of the brain, a great proportion of the brain cells represent the physical sensations and feelings of the face, hands and feet. These are high awareness areas. As you release and breathe, send energy out to the five points.

Streaming As a Way to Relax

The pro football season is six to seven months of physical violence. To stay fresh and alive, one of my clients did some streaming regularly throughout the season. Almost every day, he'd put aside ten to fifteen minutes to release and breathe and stream energy through his body. He invariably had some sore spots (an ankle, a shoulder, a hip or a thigh) that he would direct the energy to. He found the whole process energizing and recharging.

We used to get together every couple of weeks for a "power session." It consisted of his relaxing and breathing ... then streaming energy out to the five points. As he relaxed, he gradually increased the amplitude of each breath, drawing in more energy and sending more out.

At one point, he really got "connected." He was breathing rhythmically, inspirationally, and experiencing what he called "big waves rolling in." He described feeling "wonderful," as if a "sun roof opened up" in the top of his head and golden energy was streaming in and flowing through his body. When he focused on his hands, he said they were "vibrating." He described feeling so powerful that even though he was relaxed he felt as though he could punch right through a stone wall.

After he had been breathing and streaming for about fifteen minutes, his energy shifted and he became quiet. He was lying still, and breathing easily and rhythmically. A couple of minutes passed. Then I asked him to relate how he felt on a scale of one to ten (ten being great). There was a long pause, maybe half a minute ... then his quiet voice said, "ninety." This warrior found streaming a valuable, pleasurable balance to the assault and stress of his occupation. And he used it for years.

The pro season in sales, management and in most professions can be seen as eleven months of mental aggression and stress. You can use a similar streaming process (without necessarily increasing the amplitude of each breath) to help you to relax, balance and recharge ... every day.

In the course of competition, athletes often have to react suddenly to stop a ball, or puck or to avoid being hit by something or someone. The tension associated with these intense, contractive reactions is frequently *stored* in the body. Streaming is a good way for people under pressure to release feelings. Be aware that the process of releasing ... breathing ... and streaming can produce some twitching as the stored tension and stress is released.

We release some of the tension and stress we accumulate naturally, especially in processes like exercising and sleeping. Streaming is an efficient and pleasurable way to let go even more, and to keep body and mind relatively stress-free.

I recall the wife of an NHL goalie saying that sleeping with her husband was like sleeping in a war zone. Between his releasing tension naturally (twitching) and his blocking shots in his dreams, she was getting pummeled. Streaming (every day during the season) helped him clear some of that tension, and allowed both of them to experience more peaceful, restful sleep.

All of us accumulate and store tension throughout the day. Just getting to and from work can be tensing and stressful. After a rush-hour drive through Los Angeles, one of my NHL clients commented, "How do people put up with this every day? I get more uptight driving around L.A. than by playing an entire hockey game."

Streaming is very relaxing. I recommend it as *daily* relaxation therapy, anywhere from two to fifteen minutes a day, whatever feels right to you. It's a pleasurable way to release tension, recharge and balance yourself.

Streaming As a Way to Enhance Performance

Consider a speaker about to deliver what he or she believes to be an important address. Consider a golfer getting ready to make an approach shot in a close match. Consider a batter preparing himself to hit the ball. In each case, successful performers use their minds aggressively to create feelings that empower them.

What's important as the batter stands at the plate is that he sees the ball clearly and that he brings his energy into it. To do that, he prepares himself in the on-deck circle by breathing in energy and sending it out into the feet, into the hands and into the bat ... and he sends energy up into his head and eyes. He streams it out to the five points. He *feels energy* in his body. He feels this as he takes a few swings.

Bruce was a talented young man who was frustrated by his inability to express his potential. As a collegiate baseball player, his performance had been mediocre. In his first two years at the university, he hit a total of fourteen home runs, had a .230 batting average and was well on his way to setting a school strikeout record. He was so frustrated by his lack of success that he often upset himself and threw something (a bat or helmet) after one of his not-so-infrequent strikeouts. Bruce was referred to me by one of his coaches to "help him realize his potential."

When I began working with Bruce, he was a strong man who tried to hit the ball out of the park at every bat. The first thing I did was remind him to release and breathe. Then we worked with streaming. Like many strong people, he thought his strength was all in his upper body. When he tried to "muscle" the ball, he did it with his shoulders and arms. He "squeezed" too hard and struck out too much. What helped him was learning to ease up and stream energy out into the bat. (When a batter is tight and squeezes too hard, energy doesn't flow into his bat. Similarly, when a golfer presses and squeezes too hard, less energy flows into the club.) What also helped Bruce was becoming more aware of his lower body. He accomplished this by streaming energy down into his feet and developing a greater awareness of his base.

Another valuable training insight Bruce experienced was the sense of being "connected" to an unlimited supply of energy. The more he relaxed and opened up, the more energy he could draw in and stream through his body. The more he streamed energy, the more power he felt and the better he performed. We combined breathing and streaming with Bruce imagining himself swinging with ease, making good contact and hitting the ball with power. He imagined himself hitting all kinds of pitches. First, we worked with fast balls, then with curves and change-ups, pitches that demanded more patience and control. And it all seemed to help. That year, Bruce tied the NCAA record for the most home runs hit in a single season (a 300% performance increase over his previous years' statistics). He led his team to the college world series and was an All-American selection.

He was interviewed on television late in the season and asked, "How come you're suddenly hitting all these home runs? Have you been lifting weights? Did you change your diet? What are you doing differently?"

"You see," he replied with a big sweep of his hand, "there's this energy all around us. I just open up and let it flow through me." For this strong man, "muscling" became a process of breathing, streaming and easing, instead of "squeezing."

To my mind, Bruce's adjustments were as much mental as they were physical. They involved his easing up and integrating; then, realizing that he had a personal connection to an unlimited supply of energy, tapping into it and expressing that power.

Many of my clients are white-collar workers. Some wear ties that symbolically cut off their heads from their bodies. Streaming can be as effective a performance aid for them as it is for the home run hitter. It can help them to feel more integrated and "connected," both to an unlimited supply of energy and to an unlimited supply of good ideas. It builds confidence and wellbeing.

Streaming As a Way to Reduce Pain and Promote Healing

Pain is part of life for millions of people. I have spent several years working with people who had experienced significant injuries. Many of these injuries prevented their return to work for years. I assisted them in reducing pain. And streaming was one of the most effective techniques for this.

As part of the program, I would demonstrate to them how much control they had over their bodies, their "mind over matter" power. After just a few sessions of relaxation training, I'd ask the members of the group to think of streaming warm energy down into their right hands. We would monitor the temperature of that hand with biofeedback equipment. What surprised, impressed and delighted most of the group was that they could significantly raise their hand temperature by *thinking* of sending warm energy into the hand. Some could even cool the hand below the starting temperature by thinking of the hand as cold.

Relaxing and directing warmth into the hand actually affects the flow of blood (energy) into the area, increasing the temperature. Similarly, you can stream soothing, healing, relaxing energy into any part of the body, reducing pain and facilitating the healing process.

If you are a visually imaginative person, you can increase that effect by adding the dimension of color to the streaming process. Streaming a warm, soft gold or rose-colored energy into the area of dis-ease tends to increase blood flow and relaxation and is most effective for chronic aches and pains. Streaming soothing cool blue or green is more effective as an anesthetic for acute pain.

Dave was the manager of one of the most technically sophisticated clothing plants in North America. He had pushed for, selected and was supervising a very expensive, high-productivity system. And he was committed to seeing it work. In the months it took him to make the venture profitable, Dave put himself under considerable pressure. He worked very hard. He thought about his system eighteen hours a day. Then, he started to experience severe headaches, caused by constriction of the blood vessels in his head. The headaches were so intense they interfered with Dave's life and the way he related to other people's health and performance. He knew he should ease up, but he wasn't doing it. That's when we began to work.

I showed Dave two techniques. The first was to release ... breathe ... and refocus. I explained that it was a technique he could use throughout the day to stay relaxed and to keep the pressure from building up. The second was streaming. I encouraged him to take at least ten minutes twice a day to release, breathe and stream a soothing, relaxing energy though his body. When he had a headache, I told him to stream a soothing stream of energy into the headache center behind his left eye. He'd go right into the spot, ease it open and then stream a soothing, warm, pastel pink energy right into the center of the dis-ease.

Dave's motivation and drive to excel remained unchanged. However, as he began to use the "release" techniques regularly, his ability to handle the pressure increased and the headaches diminished.

Streaming is an antidote to pain and dis-ease. If you suffer from acute or chronic pain, tune into the source of your discomfort. Locate the exact spot where the tension and pain is most extreme. Explore the pain. Determine the size, shape, intensity, "color" and any other of its properties. Then relax and go deeper into the area of your discomfort.

What we resist often persists. Instead of fighting your pain, go into it. Release and breathe. Then stream a soothing, healing energy into the center of the pain. The more you can relax and tune into the center of your pain, the deeper you can go into it. The more soothing energy you can stream through it, the more the pain will diminish.

I introduced streaming to one of the Dodger pitchers I was working with. He had been troubled by a sore elbow for which he had received a variety of state-of-the-art physical therapy treatments. After streaming some cool, soothing blue energy through his sore arm for about ten minutes, he exclaimed, "My arm feels like it's vibrating. This stuff is more powerful than ultrasound."

"This stuff," I reminded him, "is your ability to release, breathe and focus *your energy.*"

The streaming process is about drawing in energy and directing or guiding it to a specific part of the body, often while under pressure or stress. It's a basic physical expression of body-mind power and control. Streaming is also a bridge to projecting your energy out into the environment. The same principles are operative in exercising that kind of control and impact.

Remember, you have a *personal* connection to an *unlimited* supply of energy.
To tap it, release … breathe … **stream**.

CHAPTER 10 TRAINING NOTES

Streaming

1. **During weeks two and three**: At the end of your daily breathing session, spend three to five *minutes* each day streaming energy out to the five points (and anywhere else you want to attend to).

   During week four: Increase the duration of your streaming sessions to 10 minutes a day.

2. **During weeks two, three and four**: Several times during the day, spend *30 seconds* to a minute streaming energy through your body. Remember, streaming can be especially effective when you're tense, tight, tired, depressed or sore.

3. Remind yourself:

   "I have a personal connection to unlimited energy."
   "Energy flows to me ... and through me."
   "I deserve to feel good."
   "I am response-able to change my feelings."

chapter eleven

BLOWING OFF
TENSION

In Chicago, I had arranged an afternoon meeting with a Mariners relief pitcher I had worked with on several occasions. When I got to his hotel room at the appointed time, I found him in a heated argument with his wife. I waited outside the room for him to extricate himself from the unpleasant exchange.

He was visibly shaken. We went back to my room, and since he was still upset, I said, "Why don't you just sit back, relax and tune into your breathing."

"Relax. I don't want to relax." The charge was still there and he roared back, "My wife's on my back. My ex-wife's on my case, and my kids are bugging me. I've got a splitting headache, and I'm scheduled to pitch tonight."

It was clear that he had to vent some of the charge he had built up, to "blow it off," before he could feel calm enough for us to get down to business. He went on to rage for another minute, then he quieted down, got into his breathing and relaxed.

Sometimes, when someone's really tense, keyed up or under pressure, simply letting go of the contraction ... releasing and breathing, doesn't "feel right" or just isn't enough. Another way to balance yourself and to get rid of tension, fear, stagnation and fatigue is to "blow some of it off." There are many ways this can be done. The pitcher's explosion was one. However, explosions are difficult to control, and they can be very hard on relationships.

Blowing off tension can be especially useful if pressure is overwhelming or if people find themselves too tense or aroused at a time when they have to perform. It's an effective technique. However, it is a safety valve procedure that focuses on the exhalation and on you being "at effect" of what's happening around you. As a general rule, blowing off tension is a poor substitute for using the situation you're in to inspire yourself (inhale) and to be more "at cause." "At cause" and "at effect" are terms I use in therapy. If you're operating "at cause," you are proactive and in charge. If you're "at effect," you are being reactive — trying to keep up.

Dick was one of the more creative and thoughtful golfers on the PGA tour. Sometimes he felt his thoughts were interfering with his smoothness and consistency. He felt he was playing "tight," so he decided to check this out. Dick put on a heart monitor and noticed that as he addressed the ball his heart rate began to accelerate rapidly. It went up to a point he considered to be outside his optimal performance range. So he devised a way of literally blowing off some of the tension.

Taking his club in both hands and holding it in front of him at eye level, Dick would draw in a breath ... then, he'd lower the club quickly while blowing out hard. Checking the monitor, he discovered that blowing off the tension in this way he could send his heart rate way down. It also blew off some of the discomfort. Then, Dick would address the ball and play the shot while his heart rate was reduced and in its optimal performance range.

Dick uses this procedure before every shot. I thought it was a bit mechanical and suggested a few modifications. However, it's a routine he says he's comfortable with ... and he's playing well. That's the bottom line.

Another approach to blowing off tension is one that's a little more dramatic and that I borrowed from the martial arts. It involves a focused, explosive expression of energy; a couple of short punches not directed at anyone but as though one is punching through an imaginary block of soft, corky wood, accompanied by a few yells or roars. There's a specific way to punch and yell that can be learned with a little coaching. However, don't let the mechanics (or lack thereof) inhibit you. Any series of four to eight crisp, short, rhythmic punches (not rushed and, again, not aimed at anyone) accompanied by deep (from the chest, not the throat), loud, unhibited yells can not only dispel tension, inhibition, tiredness and fear, it can be fun. The classic karate sound is "*keeii*," but you can use whatever sound feels right or works for you.

A kilo racer is a cyclist who rides three times around a circular track as fast as he can for one kilometer against the clock. When you're a kilo racer, you have only one chance at each competition to excel. There's only one ride at the Olympics or the World Championships. There are no practice heats, no two out of three runs. There's just one chance. To make things even more intense and high pressure, the whole race takes just over one minute to complete. There's great pressure to make every tenth of a second count. To do that, you have to come off the starting line fast, accelerate quickly and smoothly, get up to top speed and maintain it for a whole three laps.

As a race time approaches, the tension builds. Some competitors respond well to the pressure. Others get too tight. The time just before the race is ideal for blowing off excessive tension and getting into one's optimal performance-arousal range.

Curt Harnett was one of the finest kilo racers in the world. When we first met at the Pan-American Games in Venezuela, he was on the way up. "I've been training for months," he said, "and it all comes down to sixty-five seconds. I've got to make sure I'll be there." As part of his mental preparation, we worked with a variety of techniques, from a punching, yelling karate exercise that would help him to blow off some of the excessive pre-race tension to high-performance imagery and power thoughts.

In Chapter One, I described Curt Harnett as a young cyclist at the Olympics. At 19, he was the youngest competitor in the race. Yet he knew exactly what to do to prepare himself to excel. He was a power man in a power event. He knew what to do to build up his concentration and what to do to reduce tension. A couple of hours before the race, he relaxed and ran through his breathing, streaming, imagery routine (again). In the seconds just before the race, as the pressure built, Curt would straddle his bike, tune into his breathing, get focused and do a modified punch and yell technique to blow off any excessive tension. Then, he'd draw in a little more power and take off.

Curt rode a great race in the Olympics, a personal best. He led the field until the last rider beat his time. He won a silver medal.

Blowing off tension is a popular technique. I've worked with many women, both athletes and executives, who've enjoyed it. They especially seem to enjoy the opportunity, the permission and the feeling of aggression involved in blowing off tension. It can be very freeing and empowering. Blowing off tension is an expressive, assertive way to make balance that many of my clients have used for a definite "performance lift."

The key to this technique is to blow off the excess, what's undesirable, not the entire charge, then to build back up so that you're "performing" in your optimal arousal range.

This super-release principle is applicable to all of us. In counseling, clients have come in at times with considerable tension and some very strong emotions, the three principles of which are anger, fear and sadness. I talk with them about their feelings, goals and circumstances. And I remind them to relax (to release, breathe and refocus). This is the fundamental tool for coping and achieving.

Sometimes the emotional charge they're experiencing is too great for them to simply release, breathe and refocus. They're ready to explode. Sometimes their inhibition is like a stone wall, and it's limiting them. In either case, I have them blow off some tension and emotion so they can feel better and operate more effectively.

A 40-year-old businessman who was intensely angry with his partner came to see me. We talked about this problem for a few minutes, then I asked him to relax and breathe. Like the pitcher, he responded with, "I'm pissed off, and I'm not going to sit back and relax — not now." So I had him go into his anger and express *some* of it using a modification of the technique I have just described.

After he had released some of the intensity he felt, he was able to sit back, get comfortable, relax and breathe. As he breathed properly, he felt more at ease, more positive and better able to deal with his feelings and circumstances. He affirmed this, as well as a new feeling that he didn't need his partner's approval to feel good about himself. We were able to explore something of what upset him in his relationship with his partner and how there were some similarities in this to a previous significant relationship he'd had.

Had he not blown off a little of the tension and emotion, he would have been too "uptight," blocked or charged to use his experience productively. Had he blown off all the tension and emotion, he might have experienced a temporary release, but more than likely he would have lost an opportunity to enhance his self-awareness.

CHAPTER 11 TRAINING NOTES

Blowing Off Tension

It can be stressful, unhealthy and unproductive to habitually suppress or repress your feelings. Having said that, I'm reluctant to encourage people to simply blow off anger and frustration without having a therapist/counselor or responsible individual present. There's always a possibility of misinterpretation and poor judgment; the intense emotions these exercises can generate may produce a regrettable result. However, the exercise I'm going to suggest is similar to the one described in this chapter, and it's one that's effective in reducing inhibition.

1. **During weeks three and four:** Find a space where you won't be disturbing anyone. Count aloud from one to ten. Counting is a good way to increase your volume and intensity in incremental steps. Start with one being moderately loud. Increase the loudness and intensity with each number so that you are **roaring** on numbers eight through ten.

2. **During week four:** Here's an option for you. If you like, punctuate each number with a punch. The punch shouldn't be directed at anyone or anything. Instead as you punch, imagine punching through a block of soft, corky wood.

Keep increasing the amplitude of your sound.

3. Remind yourself:

"I'm the boss."

"I'm the master of my reactions."

"I can calm myself down or pump myself up."

"I enjoy expressing my energy (power, feelings)."

chapter twelve

INDIVIDUAL
DIFFERENCES

Pressure creates tension, and when you're tense you
want to get the task over as fast as possible. The more
you hurry in golf, the worse you probably will play,
which leads to even heavier pressure and greater
tension. To avoid this vicious circle, I'll take a few deep
breaths and quickly review why I'm doing what
I'm doing.
~Jack Nicklaus, PGA Champion

The pressure makes me more intent on each shot.
Pressure on the last few holes makes me play better.
~Nancy Lopez, PGA Champion

We're all different. Everyone is unique and special. Most people perform at their best by staying calm under pressure. Others thrive on pressure, and seek out challenging situations that "pump them up."

A key to facilitating performance is to discover what works for you.

A few facts of life:

1. Everyone can benefit from improving their ability to relax.

2. The most common response to pressure is to contract and tighten up.

3. The most effective antidote to performance dis-ease, whether it's in a ball game, a business conference, a concert or an exam, is to: **release ... breathe ... refocus**.

It's worth noting that a minority of my clients perform better by increasing (as opposed to decreasing) their level of emotional intensity or arousal. Their preferred response to pressure is to "pump themselves up."

TENNIS ANYONE?

Tennis was the first sport I worked with, and from a psychological point of view it's one of the most demanding. At the elite level, it can be two hours of intense competition demanding strength, speed, concentration and finesse. And it's maximum exposure. You're out there on the court alone. On a bad day in other individual sports like golf, you can slip into the anonymity of the field and disappear. In downhill ski racing, the challenge and the danger are formidable, but the event lasts only a few minutes. In contrast, tennis can be hours of confrontation with no place to hide, and no one but yourself to blame for a disappointing performance. The same breathing, release and refocusing techniques that have helped a number of budding tennis stars deal with the pressure of this complex, demanding game apply to all aspects of life.

In 1980, the Mississippi State University tennis coach, Jim Poling, came to see me. Jim was a former professional tennis player, an ex-army intelligence officer and a graduate of several "mind control" courses. He had great respect for the psychological side of the game, and asked if I would do some "mental training" with the team. I began by teaching the athletes to release and breathe. I wanted them to develop more emotional control and have greater ability to change channels on their mental TVs. We then went on to work on some "winning programing" that involved combining good playing mechanics with imagery, affirmations and power feelings.

One thing I did with the team was to develop a precompetition routine. Before each match, the players would lie down for five minutes with their eyes closed and their racquets in hand. After relaxing and breathing for a few moments, they would mentally run through every aspect of their game and imagine themselves playing well, with balance, smoothness and accuracy — making all their shots. Most of the players really enjoyed the process and found it set them up well. However, two of the eight team members didn't like it at all. They said it made them nervous. Instead of spending a few minutes being quiet and calming down, they wanted to do some energizing to "pump" themselves up. So we designed a stimulating, thigh-slapping respond-to-the-ball reaction drill for them, got them moving and encouraged them to choose some hard-driving music to listen to on their Walkmans just prior to going out onto the courts to warm up.

We also developed self-talk programs for all the players. The self-talk (see Chapter 15) we created with the two players who wanted more stimulation was very upbeat, challenging and provocative. Essentially, it was designed to evoke the feelings of high arousal that they felt gave them an edge and helped them to perform.

Half a dozen years later, I was working with the Los Angeles Kings of the NHL. In the course of my work, I made tapes for several of the players. The tapes reminded them to release and breathe. They contained both confidence-building affirmations and high-performance images repeated in a supportive, reassuring voice. The content of the affirmations and images were based on input provided by the players.

Again, most of the players enjoyed the tapes and reported that they were beneficial in helping them to feel more calm, centered and focused. However, one player called me over in the dressing room after practice one day, and said, "Doc, I've listened to the tapes a few times, and I've got to be honest with you. Before a game, I play much better if someone yells at me … and really gives me shit. That's what helps me to get going." We changed the intensity and the tone of his message accordingly.

There's an old Chinese maxim which says that *one way to reduce fear is to introduce anger*. There's no doubt this works to manipulate short-term behavior. The military has used this tactic to push soldiers beyond their fear for centuries. It's also been a standard in sport and business. In the old days, a good kick in the rear (verbally or physically) was one of the principal ways to "motivate" an athlete. However, times are changing. Coaching is becoming more of a science. The idea that more push doesn't always translate into consistent high-level performance is out there and spreading. In North

America, the practice of coaching and managing by intimidation seems to be fading about as fast as salaries are escalating.

Both pitching coaches and sales managers are increasingly aware of the importance of being reassuring and calm when dealing with players under pressure. In baseball, the goal in addressing the pitcher in "a jam" is often to help him stay focused and to prevent him from being too tense, anxious or overaroused. Coaches know that this usually translates into overthrowing and a loss of accuracy. In sales, the same anxieties generated by a slump of a slow start to a campaign often translate into overselling and lost effectiveness.

The coaching formula I usually recommend for baseball is: first, the coach takes a breath or two to calm himself ... and the pitcher ... down. Next, the coach assesses the situation (i.e., whether to leave the pitcher in the game or not). If he chooses to leave the pitcher in the game, it's important that the coach appear confident and reassuring. Lastly, the coach addresses specific positives with the performer (for example, what the pitcher can throw to get the next batter(s) out).

In most cases, that's the approach taken. However, sometimes the old style prevails — with effect. One of the premier relief pitchers in the National League was one of those rare characters who was much more responsive to scolding and intimidation than to reassurance. In the minor leagues, his manager once confided to me, "I don't know what to do with this guy. Sometimes he's out of control, but whenever I try to calm him down, reassure him or show him any kindness at all he becomes even more angry and upset."

The answer came from another pitching coach in the organization who had been shockingly successful with the young pitcher. I say shocking because when I asked the coach what he did that was so helpful to the young hurler, he replied, "I scare him. I tell him to cut the nonsense and start throwing strikes — or, I'll beat the daylights out of him."

Everyone has an optimal performance range. That's the level of emotional intensity that they perform best at. For most people, it's in the range of a mid- to moderately high level of emotional arousal. For some, it can be a little higher than that. But generally speaking, if you are either too subdued (low arousal) or too pumped up (high arousal) performance drops off.

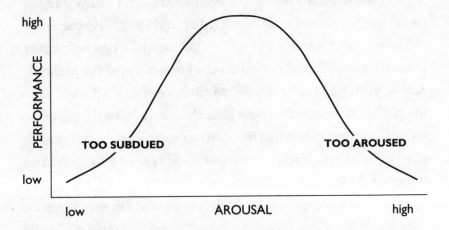

Four years after my encounter with the pitcher I described earlier in the chapter, I was watching him performing at a critical moment in the final game of the National League Championship Series. It was an extremely high-pressure situation, the ninth inning with his team up by just a run, the home crowd standing and roaring with each pitch. It was the kind of stuff that would drive almost any man's arousal level sky-high — and it was too much even for this pitcher, a raging extravert who loved to be pumped up. The result of the situation, the noise and the pressure was that he became too "pumped" and began to trying to throw the ball through the backstop. As he did, his effectiveness diminished.

It's similar in many performance fields. Commission salespeople are under a great deal of pressure to perform. During six months of coaching a Canada Life insurance sales team, I explored with the sales manager what helped his sales team deal most effectively with the pressure of a slow week or a poor month. For the most part, he advocated being supportive and focusing on the positives.

The sales manager acknowledged individual differences of the people on his team and different ways of dealing with them. He was more apt to reassure the sensitive, reserved salespeople and chide and challenge some of the more outgoing. He cited the example of an excellent salesperson who became nervous and depressed whenever her numbers dropped. "I remind her to release and breathe, then I reassure her that she's a star, and that she can best do the job by going back to the basics. [In insurance sales, that means getting on the phone, making appointments, meeting people, listening to their needs, explaining the benefits, signing the contract and getting referrals.] It's pretty much the approach I'm taking with most of my team."

In sales and in baseball, I think the single most important thing that a "coach" can do for the aspiring young professional is not just to push more technique at them (which is the tendency), but to **build self-esteem**. One of the most effective ways to build esteem is by giving people a sense of being in control. I do this by teaching them how to control the switch, to regulate emotion and change the channel — and by reminding them that they control the switch.

It's different in football, and in some facets of industry. In football and on the assembly line, it's the plan, not the individual, that's significant. It's the plan at any price, and the player must fit the plan. In baseball and sales, it's the individual that's so important. And it's the individual who must be nurtured by sensitive coaching to build the performer's self-esteem.

I told the sales manager about the relief pitcher who responded to threats and intimidation and asked him if it was his history that his salespeople responded better to confrontation than to reassurance. "Oh, there are some I have to poke a little," he replied. "Actually, I used to do more of that barnyard motivation when I first started. You know, take out the electric cattle prodder and give people a jolt to keep them moving forward. Truth is, it moves some people for a short time, but it also creates resentment. Besides, it's not the way to build a professional sales team. The majority of my sales team … stimulated by a challenge or a campaign. But there are very few people in this business who can sustain a high level of performance with threats, fear, tactics and abuse. And once you start prodding people, you often have to keep prodding to get results. Even if it did work, I wouldn't want to have to operate like that all the time."

Overarousal can be limiting in any performance area. Randy was an aspiring member of an improvisational comedy troupe I did some work with. He was a pleasant young man under some real self-imposed pressure to "make it." Like most performers, when he stepped into the spotlight and center stage Randy's arousal levels went up. On the night of his "rookie debut," they went way up. One of the results was that Randy simply forgot to "use" the people he was playing with. Curiously, what Randy experienced is the same barrel vision that sometimes limits a distraught or inexperienced quarterback under pressure. What it does to the quarterback is to limit his perspectives and compress time, making him feel like the three seconds he has to release the ball is less than two seconds. It did the same to

Randy. Not surprisingly, it reduced his effectiveness, and the effectiveness of the whole group of players.

The techniques most helpful to Randy were just what we've been describing in the first half of the book. That is, remembering to release ... and breathe (to moderate the arousal). Then imagining/experiencing himself playing with the other three people on stage — and playing with an abundance of ease and humor.

Why is it that some people perform better when they release, breathe and calm down, while others need to feel "pumped up" or stimulated to perform at their best? And why do some people thrive on high-pressure jobs such as police officers, air traffic controllers, emergency room physicians, hockey goalies or relief pitchers, when others go into emotional overload at the mere thought of a high-pressure occupation? There are a number of factors that can account for the different ways people react to pressure.

ARE YOU AN INTROVERT OR AN EXTRAVERT?

The most differentiating features of personality accounting for different styles and abilities to handle pressure and stress are **extraversion** and **introversion**. People commonly use the term extravert to refer to someone who is outgoing or stimulus-seeking and the term introvert to refer to someone who is more quiet, reserved and focused within.

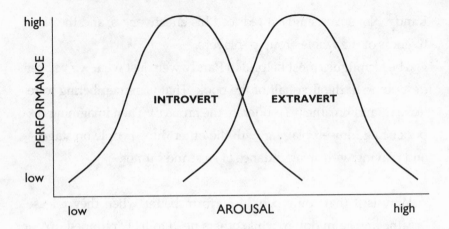

One way to explain the difference between extraverts and introverts is that introverts are more sensitive. Under normal conditions, they have a higher base level of emotional arousal than extraverts. Hence, they find any additional increase in stimulation or pressure overstimulating; they become anxious, tighten up and their performance decreases.

Extraverts, on the other hand, have a lower base level of arousal. Since they are less aroused, they are more stimulus-seeking. Many extraverts, like the relief pitcher, respond better to an increase in arousal than introverts do.

Some people have a pretty good idea of their personality style, others don't. If you want some feedback on yours, and whether you score as introverted or extraverted, one of the best tests available is the Myers Briggs Type Indicator.* I use it in my work facilitating high-level athletic performance with corporate and management teams and for treating chronic pain patients and their families.

---

*The Meyers Briggs Type indicator is available through Consulting Psychologists Press, Palo Alto, CA. Two booklets that I'd recommend are *Introduction to Type in Organizations* and *Lifestyles*. Both are by Sandra Hirsh and Jean Kummerow, and are available through Consulting Psychologists Press.

WHAT DO YOU ACTUALLY DO?

Another factor that determines appropriate levels of emotional intensity or arousal is the task or job you perform. In general, the curve that describes the relationship between emotional intensity and performance for tasks involving a fair degree of complexity and judgment (quarterbacking, golfing, pitching a baseball, interacting with people — teaching, managing, selling) is similar to the inverted U curve I discussed in relation to arousal and performance. It shows that a moderate amount of emotional intensity is necessary for people to peform a relatively complex task their best. At low levels, their performance is inferior, and at very high levels of arousal their performance of complex tasks also drops off.

For tasks of lower complexity (that's not to be confused with easy tasks like weight-lifting), there's more of a direct relationship between the two factors. That's to say, other things being equal, the more pumped up you are, the better you're likely to perform.

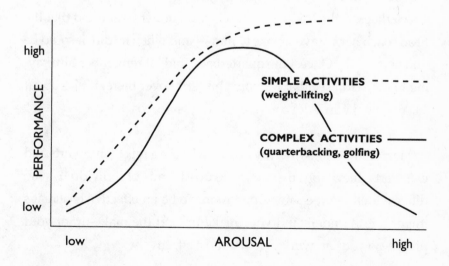

Job requirement and personality style can interact. It's a little easier for extraverts to perform in sales than introverts. However, there's no personality mold for success. What's important is that you get in touch with who you are, that you determine what works for you and that you behave accordingly.

The personality and coaching style of successful NFL coaches is extremely diverse. What is consistent is that they're all true to themselves, and that they can tune out distraction and pressure and focus on the job at hand.

I remember discussing the personality style of some of the top NFL coaches with NFL perennial All-Pro Jack Youngblood in the mid-eighties. "There's not one personality or coaching style," said Jack. "They're a collection of personality stereotypes." He went on to describe John Madden of the Raiders as the entertainer. Bill Walsh of the 49ers as the professor. Tom Landry of the Cowboys as the minister. John Robinson of the Rams as the politician. Mike Ditka of the Bears as the labor boss. And Bud Grant of the Vikings as the hunter.

Unlike extraverts like Madden and Ditka, Grant appeared to be an introvert who rarely spoke to his players. One of my clients who had quarterbacked the Vikings for three years under Grant said that the head coach hardly ever spoke to him — and when he did, it could be quite unusual. "Once," the quarterback said, "I remember him saying to me, "You see that Monarch butterfly over there. It flies about 5,000 miles a year. All I could reply was, 'sure, coach.' "

Most teams are coached by people who are a mix of introverts and extraverts. Inevitably, they're made up of a mix of individuals who differ widely on the same dimension. To be an effective coach, it's important to understand your make-up and the make-up of your players so you can work together most effectively.

In the early eighties, I worked with several players who were members of the Vancouver Canucks. One was an aggressive, extraverted veteran who thrived on provocation and confrontation, another was a young player with considerable potential who was considerably more sensitive, reserved and introverted than most hockey players.

In the same period of time, the team experienced two very different coaches. Both were intelligent, experienced hockey men. One was a sharp-tongued, aggressive-minded individual who would on occasion taunt and provoke his players. The other was a more mild-mannered, cerebral coach. What was interesting to me, working with both men, was how these two talented players responded to the two coaches. The extraverted veteran was more responsive to the more aggressive, sharp-tongued coach, who he found to be stimulating. The more sensitive, introverted player was far more responsive to the second coach, who took him aside and quietly explained what his role was and what was expected of him. Playing for the latter coach, the young player became a star. When that coach was later fired* and was followed by another extravert, the young player's performance again slipped dramatically.

TAKE STOCK

Sit down and reflect on two or three times in the recent past when you performed very well. Recall your preparation for the event and

---

*There's tremendous pressure on hockey coaches. In the NHL, they are fired faster than coaches are in the NFL, NBA or major league baseball.

the build-up to it. Recall how you felt, and what you did immediately prior to competition. There are some marked differences on what feels "right" and what facilitates different individuals.

Of all the major sports, football creates the most intense, high-pressure pre-game atmosphere. One of the things I admired about John Robinson, the Los Angeles Rams football coach, was his understanding of the different needs of his players and that he allowed them the pre-game time and space to prepare as they saw fit.

Before a game, some of the players in the Rams' dressing room could be seen sitting quietly, some with towels over their heads, mentally rehearsing their performance, listening to music, meditating — calming themselves and preparing themselves to play. Others, usually the more extraverted, would be pacing, moving restlessly, talking to themselves, and doing things to pump themselves up … including sometimes hitting a teammate or a locker. Some could be seen gathered together talking, joking, laughing.

CHAPTER 12 TRAINING NOTES

Know Thyself

Monitor your feelings. Develop a pre-performance behavior pattern that feels good and works for you. One way to do this is to recall two or three times when you performed at your best. Then, recall two or three times when your performance was disappointing. In both cases, write down as much as you can recall about how you felt on those days.

Were you confident?
Were you clear?
Were you able to focus or concentrate?

Were you calm, pumped up or nervous? (Some athletes monitor their pulse rate to determine if they were in their optimal performance range. If their heart rate is faster than what they have determined is their precompetition ideal, or if they feel too excited, they calm themselves down. On the other hand, if their heart rate is too low, or if they feel underaroused, they pump themselves up.)

Recall some of your more memorable performances.
Did you feel ready to perform or unprepared?
Were you positive or worried?
What were you thinking about?
Were you on time, early, or late?

Define a pre-performance pattern that helps you to be at your best. From here on, begin to observe your behavior when you're about to perform, including your sleep patterns, your diet and your social behavior. Remember, you can't always control the external circumstances surrounding your performance. However, when it comes to how you feel and think, it's your TV. You control the switch.

chapter thirteen

CHANGING
CHANGELS

One of my favorite stories is about two Japanese monks. Walking through town one morning, they were confronted by a beautiful young woman in a long silk kimono standing at the crossing of a muddy road. She was afraid to cross for fear of getting her lovely kimono muddied.

The first monk, seeing her dilemma, walked over to her, picked her up, carried her across the muddy road and set her down. The second monk was shocked. He stared at his companion with disbelief and anger.

All morning as they walked, the second monk glared at the first. Late in the day, they stopped for a silent meal and still the second monk stared and scowled at the first. Finally, at night as they prepared to sleep the first monk looked at the second and asked, "You look troubled my friend, what's on your mind?"

"Sure, I'm upset," exclaimed the second monk. "Back there in town this morning, in full view of everyone, you picked up a beautiful maiden and carried her across the street. We're monks. We're not

REMEMBER:

The mind is like a TV set
that watches one program at a time,
and you control the switch.

If you don't like the program,
change the channel.

If what you're watching
is not productive or pleasurable,
change the channel.

If the program is tensing,
limiting or negative,
change the channel.

Release,
breathe,
refocus.

You control
the switch.

supposed to have anything to do with beautiful women; certainly not to carry them around in public."

The first monk listened, took a breath, then replied, "I picked her up and put her down. You've been carrying her all day."

My first year consulting with the Los Angeles Rams, I was introduced to the team by the head coach, John Robinson. He spoke about the importance of the mental side of the game and that I could be a helpful resource in that area. Then I got up to speak. I wanted to keep my comments brief, describe what my work was about and have a positive impact on the group. So I said what I believe is the clearest, fastest way to communicate the operative principle of a winning mind. What I told the team was this: "The mind is like a TV set. It watches one channel at a time, and you control the switch. If you don't like the program, if what you're watching doesn't give you power or pleasure, change channels. You control the switch."

I went on to explain that my role was simply to work with people in developing winning programs and showing them how to change channels ... to control the switch.

A football team consists of a wide range of personalities and intelligence levels, yet everybody seemed to get it. They understood that tuning into winning programs would increase their possibility of success, and that they controlled the switch. The message stuck. For the next few years, whenever I was around, someone invariably made reference to what channel they or one of their teammates were experiencing. It was, "Doc, I'm tuned in." "I'm on the satellite dish. I can pick up anything." Following a good play, I heard, "That was like an instant replay of just what I'd been thinking and visualizing." And when someone miscued, it was "his set's busted" or "Man, what channel are you on?"

HOW TO CHANGE CHANNELS

"Changing channels" is about your being able to shift from one thought or feeling to another. It's about noticing that you are worrying, thinking something negative or feeling tense and uneasy … and then letting go of that limiting thought or feeling and instead focusing on competence, confidence, power and ease.

The way to change channels is the very same breathe and release technology we've been exploring in the first two sections of the book. It's first about "seeing" the negative thought or feeling, and then releasing it and taking a breath.

Releasing and breathing clears the screen. It enables you to change channels, to refocus, to introduce a new thought or "program."

At spring training, there's always enormous pressure on the younger players to perform well. Of the 150 players in most minor league camps, I would estimate that less than twenty percent will ever make it to the big leagues. The competition and the desire to impress contributes to a lot of tension and stress.

I recall working with one young player who later became a National League MVP. He was a tough ghetto kid and a real prospect. I remember him taking batting practice at the Mets' minor league complex in 1985. He had been referred to me several days earlier because he was a talented prospect and it was thought the emotional ups and downs he experienced interfered with his performance. For example, if he made an error in the field, he might allow it to affect his next few at bats.

We spent a couple of hours together, during which time I introduced him to some techniques for controlling and focusing the mind. I watched him as he was at the plate during batting practice while a former major league pitcher was throwing him a lot of off-speed "junk" pitches. In his exuberance to really hit one out, the youngster was overworking and "squeezing" too hard. He wasn't being patient. He wasn't seeing the ball. And he wasn't hitting it.

The pitching coach kept kidding him. The more the coach teased, the less he hit: he kept getting hotter and hotter, tighter and tighter, more and more frustrated. It was as though he was locked into a negative mindset and he wasn't in control. At one point, he got so angry and frustrated with his inability to hit the ball that he smashed his bat on the side of the metal batting cage.

Finally, he remembered what we had worked on several days before. At that time, I reminded him that *he* controlled the switch, and to change channels all he had to do was release ... breathe ... and refocus. He stepped out of the batter's box and took a couple of breaths. Then, with some apparent calm and composure, he stepped back to the plate and proceeded to hit four or five of the next six pitches hard.

When he finished batting, I said to him, "That's what mental toughness is about. It's controlling the switch and controlling your mind. It's not about losing your cool or breaking the batting cage." He understood. In June, July and August of 1989, he was leading the major leagues in home runs and runs batted in.

TWO KEYS TO A WINNING MIND ARE:

1. BEING ABLE TO CHANGE CHANNELS ON YOUR MENTAL TV;
2. HAVING WINNING PROGRAMS TO TUNE INTO.

Up until now, we've focused on how to change channels. Now, let's look at developing winning programs.

WINNING PROGRAMS

A winning program begins by defining clear goals that are meaningful, measurable and time-specific. Then focus on those elements that will empower you and help you to realize your goals. The elements of a successful program are:

WINNING IMAGES
POWER THOUGHTS
FEELINGS OF COMPETENCE

Our thoughts, images and feelings flow together, and they can have a profound effect on our performance.

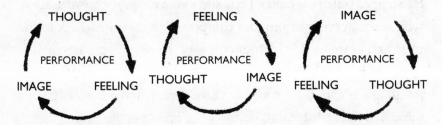

Power thoughts, high-performance images and feelings of competence generate power, increase confidence, enhance performance and stimulate wellbeing. Negative, anxious, limiting thoughts and feelings do just the opposite. They produce a biochemical reaction that stimulates more negativity and anxiety, limits performance and increases pressure.

A key to excelling under pressure is to tune out limiting thoughts and feelings, to change channels and tune into winning programs and the elements of success. These elements are discussed in the next three chapters.

The very act of defining and setting goals produces pressure. However, one of life's joys is to overcome and succeed in the face of meaningful challenges. Having a clear sense of where you are going, setting a date and time as to when you'll get there and then scheduling your course of action along the way can provide a sense of order and direction and reduce some of the stress and pressure we all experience when we invest in realizing our goals.

What Programs Limit You? FEAR ... PAIN ... DIFFICULTY.

One of the first things I do with a client is to define what it is they want to create or make happen. A second thing to determine is what images, thoughts and feelings come to mind that limit them as they perform.

What follows is a remarkable story about cycling and Olympic preparation that has relevance to us all.

In 1984 and 1988, I worked with the Canadian cycling team in preparation for the Olympic Games. In 1988, one of the groups I worked with were the TTT riders. TTT stands for team time trial. This is an event where four men ride down the highway in a straight line one behind another for 100 kilometers, racing against the clock. The first rider who encounters most of the wind resistance and sets the pace expends twenty-five percent more energy than the rest. After about forty seconds to a minute in the lead, he tires, then slips back to fourth and the second rider moves up to first. After forty seconds to a minute, he tires and slips back to fourth, and the next rider moves to the lead. And so it goes, a grueling high-speed race across the countryside, continuously alternating the lead ... with each rider pressing to maintain the pace.

In preparation for the 1988 Olympics, I worked with the TTT riders for a week at the beginning of their season in early March, showing them techniques for greater ease, focus and control. Then they went off to train and race in Texas, Britain, Belgium, Germany and in the Rockies. When I met them again in British Columbia in early July, they were in excellent shape. They were very well coached and well conditioned, and they were riding very good equipment. For a sport psychologist that's ideal. You can influence the psyche of an athlete who's not in very good shape, but in a physically demanding 100-kilometer race, having motivation without physical condition wouldn't make much of a difference. However, when athletes are both physically and technically prepared, getting them "out of their minds" about what they can't do can make a tremendous difference. That's what I set out to do.

Once the Olympic team had been selected by the cycling association, the Olympic committee (an independent body) must approve the selection. Their job is to ensure that the people sent to the games are competitive, and they won't send performers who are not up to world standards.

In the TTT, the Canadian best-ever (record) time was two hours, six minutes and forty seconds. The Olympic committee set a standard of 2:05:30. In effect, they said to these prospective Olympians, either you take a minute and ten seconds off your best-ever time, or you are not going to the Olympics. That was the challenge.

As usual, I began by showing them how to release and breathe: to feel good and to control the switch. We worked individually and in groups. As the riders became more relaxed and focused I asked them what thoughts, images and feelings ("programs") they had when they rode that were limiting to them. Essentially, they described three limiting "programs." They had to do with fear, pain and difficulty. At the time I thought their response was specific to cyclists. Later, I realized it applies to us all.

Fear. The fear the riders spoke about was a fear of losing control, a fear of breaking down, a fear of failure, a fear of embarrassment and the fear of crashing and injury. For most of us, fear is a high-frequency performance thought, one that can mobilize you for action, or cause contraction, limit breathing and cut down power.

Pain. A second limiting program was pain. The pain experienced in cycling is a physical pain so intense at times that a rider can't continue. Some even pass out on their bicycles. The pain most of us are apt to experience in relation to performance is a psychic pain. One that threatens the ego and causes contraction, limits breathing and cuts down power.

Difficulty. The third limiting program is difficulty — "It's hard." Again, under the circumstances, thoughts and feelings like "this is hard," "it's impossible," "I can't do it" also cause contraction, limit breathing and cut down down power.

I had each rider define a single thought that he could tune into whenever he experienced fear, pain or difficulty. The thought was to be a simple, powerful one ... something that was personally meaningful and that stimulated a feeling and an image that gave them power. It had to be simple and brief. The stress and fatigue of the race expresses itself like static and snow on a TV set, and we wanted a stimulus word or program that would be comprehensible and useful under intense pressure.

Each rider selected a different word. Brian, the team's leading rider, chose the word "more." Whenever he experienced pain, fatigue or self-doubt, he would think "more," and push a little harder, a little longer or a little faster. Yvon chose the word "smooth." He was a big man who knew that under pressure he'd often tighten up and end up having to work harder to accomplish the same result. Chris chose the word "machine." He wanted to be inhuman and impervious to pain, doubt and difficulty. Whenever he noticed himself tuning into a limiting thought or feeling, Chris would take a breath, draw in energy, turn the wheel and accelerate. Dave chose the word "fast." It sparked in him the image to be lighter, tougher, more aggressive and streamlined. He brought that program to mind whenever he felt stressed.

The case of one of the alternate team riders was different again. He didn't perform well when he rode for the national team. When he rode for his club, he was daring and aggressive. But as soon as he put on the national team jersey, he became tentative and defensive. Instead of "going for it," his focus became "don't make a mistake." Instead of projecting his mind forward and out along the course, he would focus downward, count his pedal revolutions and make sure he didn't pull less than his share. It was a matter of overconditioning. He had been trained that more than anything else "don't let them down," "they're watching you" and "they're counting on you." His focus was the ubiquitous "them." Consequently, the program he selected to focus on was "fuck 'em." Whenever he'd start to feel himself tighten up and think negatively, he'd take a breath, draw in power, think "fuck 'em," and turn the wheel.

An amusing sidelight to all the above is that I had each of the riders "words" written and stuck onto the back of the seat of the bicycle immediately in front of them so that as they rode (close behind each other) they would have a visual reminder of their program. The Olympic trial was held on a blocked off section of the Trans-Canada

Highway outside of Vancouver. Prior to the race, a crowd of cycling enthusiasts, friends and supporters milled around examining the state-of-the-art bicycles. With curiosity, they read the words on the back of each seat, "more," "smooth," "machine," "fast," … and then "fuck em." On seeing the last stimulus, the spectators would inevitably do a double-take and look at the rider attached to the bike. Then they either smiled or shook their head. The rider inevitably flushed, and said, "It's not my word," But of course, no one had any idea what he was referring to.

What makes the story particularly interesting is the bottom line. The riders went out at a fast pace and stayed focused and aggressive throughout the race. Dave, Chris and Yvon all mentioned to me afterwards that they were hurting, or thought "I can't do it. I can't go on." And when they noticed themselves tuning into that feeling or thought they remembered to go deeper into their breathing, to turn the wheel, to change channels, to generate more power and to refocus on their program — their word. The end result was they rode the 100-kilometer distance in 1 hour, 51 minutes and 10 seconds. Their time was *15 minutes and 30 seconds faster than the previous Canadian record*, an unofficial world record in that event.

What's remarkable is that this wasn't a new team of superstars imported from another part of the planet. Three of the four riders had been a part of the team that set the 2:06:40 mark the year before. What was different now was that all the keys were in place. They were well coached. That's to say, the right people had been selected, they knew what to do and they were in good shape. Then they were trained to be aggressive with their minds, to change channels in the face of limiting thoughts and feelings and to stay tuned into winning programs.

REFOCUSING

———

———————

Intention is a quality of a winning mind.
Intention means "to stretch out for,"
to stream energy
into clear, positive images and power thoughts.

A winning mind has the ability,
even under intense pressure,
to tune out dis-ease, limitation and negativity
and focus instead on ease, power and possibility.

It's an ability you can enhance with training.

———————

chapter fourteen

HIGH-PERFORMANCE
IMAGERY

~ Imagine yourself surrounded by space,
   the space of infinite possibility.
~ To be successful in that space
   it's important to have a clear sensory impression.
~ The brain works on sensory impressions ... or images.
~ Imagine something you believe in
   and that's meaningful to you.

~ To excel, project your image
   into the space of possibility
   and hold it there.
~ As you do, the atoms and molecules in the space begin to reso-
   nate in harmony with your image.

~ If your thoughts or images are unclear
   or charged with anxiety and anger,
   the space will reflect confusion and fear.

~ Excellence is about creating clear, meaningful sensory
   impressions,
   expressing them without fear,
   acting on them
   and staying focused on them as they manifest.

Imagination is the most powerful quality of the mind. It can be a force that empowers you to excellence ... or a force that limits you. One of the easiest ways to avoid the distraction of pressure is to have a clear mental picture of what it is that you want to do, to have, or to be, tune into it, and work at making that image a reality.

Try this simple experiment. Imagine yourself feeling very hungry. You haven't eaten all day. Someone hands you a plump, juicy navel orange. Imagine yourself admiring its deep orange color and the texture of its skin. You smell its aroma. As you peel the orange, its thick pulpy skin comes away easily. It's ripe and juicy. You break off a section of the fruit and pop it into your mouth. As you bite into the piece of orange, its sweet, tart, delicious juice instantly fills your mouth. Imagine actually biting into the orange. Notice yourself starting to salivate.

Almost everyone has had the experience of imagining themselves eating something tasty, imagining a hot, sexually arousing scene, imagining something frightening, or something very relaxing, and noticing a physiological response to their imagery. What it's important to understand is that *the mind doesn't distinguish what is real from what is imagined*. It simply reacts to the mental pictures you focus on. Effective imagination is an extension of the streaming process. In streaming, we breathe in energy and send/allow it to flow out through the body. In effective imagination, we draw in energy and send out impressions out beyond the body into the realm of possibility.

Three ways you can use effective imagination to help you excel under pressure are:

1. mental rehearsal;
2. the use of focal images;
3. imagining yourself as having achieved your goal.

MENTAL REHEARSAL means imagining yourself performing and excelling at the specific thing(s) you want to do or be.

If you're a golfer, image yourself hitting the perfect shot. See the spot you're hitting to. See the trajectory of the ball flying to that spot. Experience yourself with a grooved swing, smooth, relaxed, head on the ball, hitting it sweet. If other thoughts or images come to mind, release them, take a breath, clear the screen and refocus on the sensory impression of striking the perfect golf shot.

Whether you are in sport or business, there's more energy and enjoyment in seeing yourself as an effective coach or player. Imagine yourself with clear goals, knowing specifically what has to be done, being organized, communicating clearly and confidently and providing constructive feedback. See yourself as positive and being understood. As other images appear on your mental TV, don't let them distract you or erode your confidence. Instead, relax, clear the screen … and once again see yourself as calm, providing clear direction, informative feedback and getting results.

If you are in the process of writing something important, see your-self sitting comfortably with a clear concept of what you want to communicate. Imagine yourself personally connected to an unlim-ited supply of good ideas. Imagine that an abundance of clear thoughts and descriptive words and phrases are about to flow to you. Imagine expressing yourself well. If you feel stuck or blocked, avoid being self-critical: instead, release and breathe, clear the screen and open up to possibility. Imagine energy and ideas streaming to you and through you.

Three directives suggested by the above examples are:

1. be as clear as you can about what you want to do or be;
2. relax (release and breathe);
3. focus on the positive image of you excelling (regardless of any pressure).

Here are seven suggestions for mentally rehearsing your success and increasing your resistance to pressure and stress.

1. Define What You Want. Uncertainty is stressful. One way to increase success and reduce stress is to create clear images of what you want to be, do and achieve, and to stay tuned into these images. They're like radar that helps a ship to navigate through the fog, the dark, and in rough seas.

Again, define exactly what it is you want to experience. Be specific. Script it ... write it down. Then do some constructive daydreaming. Project or stream your energy into the images of what you want to create. As you do, your images will begin to manifest. Whenever you feel discouraged or negative and find yourself thinking "no way," "what if" or "yeah, but," release ... breathe ... and refocus on your goal(s) and stream energy into the images of what you want to create.

Nowhere is there more job insecurity and pressure to perform than in professional sport. In pro sport, the mindset is, "you're only as good as your last game." One way a pro football team deals with the uncertainty of weekly challenge is to set clear goals, define specifically what has to be done, create a game plan, then *mentally* and physically rehearse successful execution of that plan ... again, again and again ... until dealing with uncertainty and adjusting to the unexpected is something that is almost routine.

2. Relax ... Then Image. Whenever possible, release and breathe *before* putting your creative imagination to work for you. As you do, the quality of your thoughts and images will become stronger, clearer and more positive. Your sense of what's possible will increase and your ability to make these thoughts and images a physical reality will also improve.

Just taking a few moments to relax and breathe will make it easier for you to imagine yourself at your best. In sport, that may mean being faster, smarter, stronger, jumping higher, hitting further, throwing better. In life, it's having more awareness, more time, more patience, communicating more effectively and having more impact.

Before making a "challenging" phone call, take a breath or two, release unnecessary tension. Get into your optimal arousal zone. Imagine yourself calm, confident, focused and communicating effectively. Then, make the call.

3. Be Positive. Human nature is fascinating. A football player can catch five passes in a game and drop one. Too often, what he'll tune into is the image of the pass he dropped ... and that can be limiting.

Bobby Duckworth, a veteran NFL receiver, described the pressure to me. "What's tough is not simply running a pattern and catching the ball. It's running the pattern and catching the ball after 60,000 people in the stadium, your teammates and the coaching staff watched you drop the last one."

To be a consistent high-level performer, it's essential that you maintain a clear, positive image of what you want to be or do ... and that you stay focused on it. The only value in tuning into the negative, into something that didn't work, is to determine what you can do to improve in your performance. Once you're clear about that, mentally rehearse the positive.

If your sales or marketing presentation went poorly, it's not pleasurable or cost effective to keep replaying that tape in your mind ... or to keep running yourself down. That simply reinforces the negative and intensifies the pressure. Instead, review your imagery carefully with a thought to improving your technique. Look at all the elements. Were you well organized? Were you clear about what you wanted to say? Did you hit the main points? (There should no more than three.) Were you composed? Relaxed? How did you use your time? Determine what things you want to see more of, and less of, in your presentation. Then work on strengthening these elements. Repeatedly imagine yourself making your presentation with all the qualities and impact you want to express.

It's the same in golf. I know several PGA tour golfers who after missing a shot will simply "clear the screen." They'll consciously relax and erase the tension and negativity associated with the undesirable shot. They imagine themselves replaying their last shot perfectly. Then they move on to play the next shot.

4. Easy First. Move from what's easy to what's challenging. Mental training, like most forms of practice, works best when you begin by imagining yourself excelling at some activity you're comfortable with, something you've already been successful at, something easy. Then move on to something more challenging.

Cindy was a junior world champion figure skater. When I introduced mental rehearsal to her, she began by imagining herself performing split and double jumps, the parts of her routine she performed with ease, grace and joy. When she could imagine herself doing that part of her program to her satisfaction, then she went on to mentally rehearsing herself excelling at four triple jumps, which were the most demanding part of her program.

5. Create Winning Movies. Make your imagery dynamic ... like a movie (as opposed to a photograph). Be the star in that mental movie. The mind is limitless in its ability to image. Don't allow pressure to limit your positive image of yourself. And don't be the spectator watching yourself from the stands. Be a response-able player. Be the director. You can stop the film, edit it, speed it up, slow it down. Do whatever is necessary to imagine yourself as you want to be, whether that's being technically perfect, more patient, more focused, more at ease, or all of the above. You control the switch.

When I taught counseling and interviewing techniques to university graduate students, I would often ask them to listen to audiotapes of various therapeutic interactions. Sometimes the tapes were of experienced professionals in session; sometimes they were of the students themselves in training. What made the exercise especially valuable was stopping the tape every few moments and reminding the students to release and breathe (to "stay open"). As we slowed down the interaction, we were better able to evaluate what was going on, and to imagine alternatives. Through this process of releasing, breathing and editing, the students became more aware of what was being said (including the feelings behind the words) and more aware of the options open to them as effective counselors.

6. Keep it Brief. You don't have to imagine the entire performance (the whole eighteen holes). The idea is to reduce pressure and stress, not to increase it. Simply image segments (single shots) of yourself excelling under pressure. One way to keep the rehearsal alive is to keep it brief.

The marathoner doesn't have to mentally rehearse the entire two-and-a-half hours of racing. He or she can benefit more by imagining segments or flashes; three- to five-second highlights. What's important is that they imagine themselves running with ease, lightness, rhythm, good technique ... being able to let go of pain and muscular tension. You can run similar *highlights* of things you want to reinforce in mini-training periods throughout the day.

Repetition builds strength. One way to build up physical strength is simply to select an appropriate exercise and do a large number of repetitions. Similarly, to increase your mental strength, define a few simple, appropriate images (sensory impressions with direction and meaning) and then repeatedly focus on them. Practice clearing the screen on your mental TV and refocusing on high-performance images throughout the day. *Use pressure* or a tense moment as a stimulus to refocus on a positive image. Eventually, with conscious practice, the behavior of imaging the positive will develop enough response strength so that even under intense pressure and uncertainty you'll automatically tune into these supportive images.

7. Use All the Senses. Make your imagery and mental rehearsal *multisensory*. Most people are strongly visual and many think imagery is purely a visual phenomenon. The truth is, you can benefit by incorporating all of the sensory cues in imagining your performance. See it, hear it, feel it and, when appropriate, smell and taste it.

The start of any competition or race is often the time when pressure is very intense. One way to facilitate yourself during this high-pressure period is to mentally rehearse "great starts."

Jenny was an American national swimmer with good imagery skills. She came to see me at the beginning of her sophomore year at UCLA. She wanted something to enhance her performance. One of the things we worked with was multisensory imagery to improve her starts. To do this, Jenny would relax and breathe, then she would tune into the image of a specific of competition. She would *visualize* the pool, the water, the floats, the scoreboard and the competitors. She'd *hear* the crowd, the P.A. and the echos.

She would *smell* the chlorine. She would *feel* her pre-race "nerves," the tension in her shoulders, which she'd release. She'd experience herself breathing in power and streaming it through her body. Then she would change channels. She felt her feet on the blocks as "cat's feet." She would imagine herself like a powerful, hungry lion ready to spring. Then she'd lower her gaze, narrow her focus and shift to sound. She would tune into the voice of the starter, "swimmers take your marks" ... she could anticipate the starting "bleep," actually hear it as it sounded, and feel herself springing out, "hitting the hole" perfectly, gliding through the water, "breaking out," starting to stretch and pull with power ... imagining a great start. After Jenny defined the elements of her starts and then began to mentally rehearse them, the pressure became more manageable and her starts improved dramatically.

Jenny came to see me again at the start of the following year. She hadn't raced in a couple of months and she was facing her first big meet of the new season, against three top teams and a field that included an Olympic medalist. She volunteered that she didn't feel confident. We talked about her event, the 100-meter freestyle, and I asked, "What's the world record in that event?"

She quoted the time.

"Is there a time in the 100 that's your goal for the season?" I asked.

She quoted another time.

"What is your personal best at that distance?" I enquired.

Again, she mentioned a time.

Then I asked her, "What do you have to do to achieve your goal?"

"Work harder," she replied.

"That's too general," I said. "It doesn't provide us with a specific direction. Jenny, what's important is to become more aware of what actually has to change in the way you swim your race for you to be at your best."

There was a pause.

"Check it out," I said. "Imagine the race. First, see the start. [I waited a few seconds.] See yourself going out. Imagine the turn. Imagine the finish. Now, tell me, what has to change for you to swim at a world-class pace? Be specific."

Still, there was silence, so I asked, "How are your starts?"

"They're good," she replied. (As I mentioned, she had worked hard at mastering her starts the year before.)

"What about your turns?"

"They're okay," she said confidently.

"And your finish?"

"I finish strong."

"Then what's got to change?" I pressed.

"It's the fist fifty meters," she answered. "I go out too slow."

"Why?" I asked her.

"Because I'm afraid." she replied.

"Afraid of what?"

"I'm afraid that if I go out very fast, I won't have enough to finish strong."

"Well, that's reasonable," I said. "It's reasonable to be conservative if you're afraid of running out of gas." After waiting a moment, I added, "But to be the best in the world or the best you can be, you have to go beyond reason. You have to be *unreasonable*."

I explained to Jenny that people only tap a small percentage of their resources and that most of us are capable of significant performance increments just by changing our minds. I assured her that if she went beyond what was reasonable, if she really went for it, nine times out of ten she would have enough to finish strong. And, if she experienced that one time in ten when she could have performed better, then she'd know exactly what to work on in training to be more competitive.

"This weekend in the big meet," I said, "go out very fast. Be the first to the wall [fifty meters], hit a great turn, and then finish fast and strong. Use the pressure of the meet. Channel that extra energy and anxiety into an image of you that is unreasonably fast."

People under pressure often contract their imagination as well as their muscles. Jenny preferred to think positively and she found the directive to be "unreasonable" exciting. Since we had done a considerable amount of mental training in the past, I simply asked her to do some quality mental rehearsal. Her homework assignment for the week was to spend fifteen minutes a day imagining herself getting off to a quick, explosive start ("like a powerful, hungry lion") ... going out at unreasonably fast pace, swimming smoothly, with good technique ("stretching out, pulling all the way through, kicking with turbo legs") ... hitting a great turn ("'power push and glide") ... and then accelerating to the finish (more "stretch, pull, turbo legs") ...

and closing fast ("like a shark"). The watchwords to support her imagery were "smooth, fast, technique, shark" and "unreasonable."

Several days later, I saw her at the meet just before the race. She
seemed confident and focused. She gave me a big smile, slapped my
hand and shouted, "UNREASONABLE!"

In the race, Jenny got off to an excellent start. She went out very
fast and was the first to the wall. She hit a good turn and had the lead.
Then the Olympic medalist caught her and they sprinted stroke for
stroke to the finish. It was a bang, bang finish. The Olympian won the
race by 1/100th of a second. However, Jenny was also a winner. She
swam a great race, a personal best. In the second weekend of the new
seasons, she achieved her seasonal goal. And she did it not by focusing on fear and limitation but by being positive, clear and willing to
experience herself as unreasonably fast.

Jenny went on to have wonderful year. She captained the UCLA
swim team to a winning season, set a school record in the fifty meter
freestyle and was invited to the Olympic trials. She also did well in
school, maintained an active social life and learned a little more
about the power of the mind and her ability to make things happen
by projecting her energy into images of things being possible, then
acting to realize them.

About the same time that I was working with Jenny, I began consulting with three directors of a midwestern manufacturing firm. As
a company, they were performing poorly. Their annual sales were
way down, and they were under intense pressure to produce ... or
go out of business.

I began by asking them the same question I had asked Jenny,
"What has to change in the way you're performing for you to achieve

your goals?" Their initial response was similar to Jenny's. "We have to work harder."

"That's too vague," I relied. "What I want to know is what actually has to change in the way you operate your business for you to excel?"

They were silent.

"Is it design, operations, marketing or sales? What has to improve?" I asked.

"It's sales," they replied in unison.

I explained that I wasn't an expert on sales, but that they knew what had to change for them to sell more efficiently. "Is there a market for your product? Do you feel good about your line? Are you in tune with what people need and want? Is the territory too big or too small? Do you have a large enough sales force? Is it a matter of timing? Follow-up? How's your pricing? Again, what has to change for you to really excel in the marketplace?"

"I think the main problem is that we don't get out and get the business early enough," said one of the directors.

"Why not?" I asked.

"Well, there are a number of things we could say," he explained. "But to be perfectly frank, I guess we just didn't believe that it would make a significant difference, and we simply weren't willing to pay the price."

"That's reasonable," I remarked. "Why rush if the mental picture you have of the company and the market is one of limited possibility and little or no change? However, if you want to generate new possibilities and realize your potential, it's essential that you change your self-image, and your basic impressions of the company and the marketplace."

I went on to say, "success begins with motivation and an *image*, a clear sensory impression of what you want to be or achieve. Without that image, movement is limited. To create change, begin by defining what it is you want to accomplish or be. Then imagine yourself doing it. Imagine yourself out in the field early, optimistic, aggressive, successful, creating an unreasonable amount of new business. Then work at making that image a reality."

As I said in the last chapter, there's a performance cycle that links our images to our thoughts and actions. This cycle shapes our behavior. Mental rehearsal is a way into the cycle. By streaming or projecting energy into our mental images, we stimulate positive thought and action and make incredible things happen.

~ To mentally rehearse your success, define a goal.
~ Next, relax and breathe.
~ Then image yourself doing/being it.
~ Create images that are positive, progressive, brief and alive.

FOCAL IMAGES. A second way to use imagery to increase your immunity to pressure and stress is to create and use images that evoke in you feelings and qualities that you want to bring to the moment.

If you are overstimulated or too highly aroused, you might derive a sense of calm, patience and ease from the image of "a rock" or "a wave." If you want to experience "a lift" or to feel more aggressive, the image of a tiger may be more effective. In this latter vein, many people use animal images to reduce fear and anxiety and to stimulate and reinforce certain performance features they want to express.

The specific animals they select vary according to individual differences, personal preferences and the job at hand. One feature that the animals all have in common is that *under pressure they don't worry ... they simply perform*. Some of the animals my clients have used include: tigers, lions, panthers, cheetahs, bears, wolves, horses, deer, sharks, dolphins, orcas, falcons, eagles and snakes.

Doug was a two-time Olympic wrestler and a North American champion. Still, he was too tense and thoughtful, and took too much time to get going in his matches. To win at the world level, he knew he had to be more aggressive from the start. He wanted something he could focus on that would stimulate him to greater intensity and a more instant attack. We came up with the image of a "pit bull," an animal he liked and admired for its aggressiveness and tenacity. He incorporated that image into his mental preparation.

An NFL linebacker used the image of a tiger as a model of intensity, explosion and spring. His teammate, a running back, used the image of a horse for more power and breakaway speed. An NHL goalie used the image of a cat for quickness and balance. Swimmers have used images of sharks and dolphins to give themselves more finish and grace. Focusing on these images not only heightens certain performance elements, it also reinforces confidence, particularly under pressure.

Of course, there are more than just animal images that you can use. One of my favorite images for people trying to make a point is that of a whip.

It's late in the game. The score is tied and there are runners on base. Instead of tuning into the pressure, the pitcher looks in at the catcher for a sign and takes a breath. He feels strong and loose. He imagines his arm like a huge bull whip ... slowly, smoothly he draws the whip back ... and up. Free through the shoulder, he stretches it way up and out … accelerating … he snaps off a good pitch. The same analogue of starting slow and smooth and then accelerating to a peak applies in many communications areas, including sales and entertainment.

Whether you're pitching baseballs or ideas, you can use images for more ease, more impact and more control. Ron, a film producer and writer, was "overinvolved" in a project he had been working on for almost twelve years. After several abortive attempts to make the film, it finally looked as if his "life's work" was going to be made, and with a $40-million budget. Sounds great, but after years of anxiety (that he allowed to upset his health and marriage) he was so invested in the success of the film that he would react emotionally and explosively to any idea or change that he thought was inappropriate. He was a brilliant, caring individual who wanted to contribute; however, his frantic behavior, though understandable, was counterproductive. It alienated many of his coworkers, including the director, the others writers and some of the cast. To make matters worse, his dis-ease was also adversely affecting his health.

Ron said his goal was to participate in and contribute to the success of the picture. To help him communicate more effectively, I began by showing him how to exercise some pscyho-physical control, "to control the switch." To do that, we worked with breathing and release techniques. Then I gave Ron the image of "a rock" to focus on. I told him, "You're a rock. You're capable of a strong, calm, positive presence." Whenever Ron was in conference for the film, I encouraged him to focus on his breathing and think, "I'm a rock. I'm unaffected by each ripple and wave. I'm a solid, positive presence. Just my being here makes a difference."

He enjoyed the feeling and the image. He worked with his imagery and his breathing. As he gave himself time for the breath (the waves) to come in … and go out, he became more patient. He imagined having a personal connection to an unlimited supply of energy and that with each breath he was drawing some of it in. He transformed his impulse to act out with one to breathe in. And he imagined himself as a rock, unaffected by the waves, solid, calm, all-knowing, with people sitting comfortably in his presence. As Ron relaxed, breathed and imagined himself as a rock, he became easier to listen to. He eased up, and once again people began to seek out his opinion.

Three more guidelines for using your focal imagery effectively are:

1. Image Something You Want To Identify With. One company president used the image of "General Patton" to stimulate his performance. When I asked him why he chose Patton as a performance stimulus, he said, "Patton was incredibly well organized. His trademark was excellent preparation, a good game plan, speed, follow-through and the ability to "run them down." That image worked for him. With the shift in business from authoritarian football-type management to more people-oriented basketball-type team play, it's important to consider the overall impact that a "Patton-type" stimulus might have on enhancing performance. For *some* groups or teams, it's ideal.

An NFL coach referred to one of his players (a wide receiver) by the name of an NBA forward that he (the coach) admired for his scrappy, aggressive play. These were qualities that the coach wanted to strengthen in the receiver's response repertoire. The receiver, however, saw that NBA player as a clumsy hacker with no finesse. It was an image that he didn't want to identify with, and consequently the coach's message was ineffective.

Because of the obvious parallels between sport and business and since many corporate performers enjoy identifying with the competitive mentality of world-class sport, I often use sport images to stimulate a certain bottom-line awareness.

A talented young marketing executive was in the habit of waiting for things to happen. At times, it seemed like he almost expected others to do ground work before he would follow through. He was an avid basketball fan, so the president and I came up with the appropriate basketball imagery to define his corporate role and what was expected of him. We told him that he had been playing the game like a center, "posting up," waiting for someone else to bring up the ball and pass to him (whereupon he was effective at finishing the play).

We explained that what was required of him was to play more like a "point guard" — like a quarterback on the floor. When it came to marketing, he was responsible for bringing up the ball, reading the situation, calling the play and making things happen. The image of the point guard helped him understand his role. He could relate to it, he enjoyed identifying with it and his performance fell more in line with that expectation.

2. Like Mental Rehearsal, Focal Images Should Be Brief. To be maximally effective, a stimulating image should be something you can access simply by taking a breath and tuning into it, (for example, Patton, point guard, rock, light or tiger).

One Ram linebacker took a moment out of practice to ask, "What can you give me that would work in a one-on-one situation, just me and the ball carrier in the open field? I want something that reacts in an instant. If I've got to stop and think about it, he's gone."

"Think tiger," I replied. "Think of the image of a tiger springing at a man and driving him to the ground." He liked the image. It gave him just the feeling he was looking for.

An elementary school teacher asked what image she could use when she was feeling particularly stressed, tired, frustrated and caught up in being the class disciplinarian.

"What is it you see as important about what you do?" I asked her.

"I think I contribute to greater possibility in their futures," she answered.

"How could you image that?" I asked.

She thought for a while, then she said, "I give them light."

"Okay," I said, "then image yourself with the light of the sun inside you, and you sharing your light."

She liked the image. She felt it gave both her and the children what they needed.

3. Enrich Your Images With Feeling. Just as method actors are taught to use images to elicit feelings that enhance their performance, you can use images to draw on feelings that reduce anxiety to reinforce some positive quality of your performance.

Waves are an image I frequently use to help people experience feelings of rhythm, consistency, power and calm. What I ask them to do is to create these feelings by tuning into their breathing in different ways (Chapters 2-5), then bring the feeling into whatever they do. In essence, I encourage them to be like the waves as they perform.

"Big cat" images represent another series of feelings that I like to use. I suggested the image of a lion to one of the world's top shot putters. He used it in a technical way to stimulate more spring and (vertical) explosiveness in tossing the sixteen-pound steel ball. As part of his preparation and training, I encouraged him to think, feel and react more like a lion.

At one point in his preparation, he asked me whether or not I thought he should focus on the other competitors during competition. Meets can be lengthy, intense affairs where opponents often try to "psyche each other out." "Imagine you're a hungry lion," I said. "A hungry lion's main focus is the game [the deer] out there and getting it." And, since I knew him to be overly conscious of the competition, I added, "Whether a lion looks at the other lions or not doesn't really matter. What's more important is that you stay with the feeling and the focus of the powerful lion you are, and then express it."

At another point in training, we were winding down a luncheon meeting when the athlete ordered a rich, creamy dessert. "Lions don't eat junk," I commented. "If you're really serious about realizing your goals and being a lion, live like one." He looked at me, smiled and then canceled dessert. His involvement with the image gave him a perspective as well as the big cat explosiveness he wanted.

Escape. Many pain and stress-reduction programs encourage people to take a half an hour "break" in their daily lives to relax and imagine themselves in some special favorite place, *a mental retreat* where they can escape the stresses and pressures of life. For some people, that means imagining themselves relaxing by a mirror-calm mountain lake where they used to go as a child, or sitting peacefully watching the waves on a quiet beach. Others create a special fantasy spot where they feel secure and at peace. Escaping to any of these imagined retreats can provide a pleasant and stress-reducing respite, and as such it's beneficial. However, there's some evidence from studies of pain to suggest that while most people attempt to deal with "too much" by tuning into something else, those who handle pain and pressure most effectively are able to release and move into it.

Our focus is on performing under pressure and in providing a technology that will enable you to have more ease and impact in the moment *while* doing whatever it is that you do.

IMAGINE YOURSELF AS SUCCESSFUL. A third kind of imagery that you can use to help you perform under pressure is to imagine yourself as if you've already achieved your goal(s). Basically, this involves imagining yourself as the person you want to be. Seeing yourself with all the qualities: the confidence, composure, skills, awareness and work habits you aspire to, and then bringing this sense of yourself to your situation and to the moment.

When I was in college, I was fortunate to play football on a team that won a national championship. I was a back-up player who, because of injuries, became a starter midway through the season. To improve my timing, I recall having to do some extra work with the quarterback after the team's regular practice session. The quarterback was a major factor in our team's success. He was an outstanding all-conference player and the undisputed team leader. I admired his confidence and self-assurance. Then one afternoon he gave me a clue to its origins. In a quiet moment after one of our practice sessions on a cold, muddy field, I remember the veteran passing on the following advice to me. He said, "When I was a kid, my father told me that if I wanted to be the best player on the field I should imagine myself as the best. I should think and act like I'm the best out there … and then maybe that's what I'd become. Well, so far his advice has worked out pretty well."

To this day, I don't know if he imparted that bit of wisdom to shore up a rookie's confidence and encourage me to focus on the positive, or just to share something that had been meaningful for him. What I do know is that successful people in many fields have told me that their ability to hold on to the image of themselves as a winner has helped them through the innumerable obstacles and pressures they encountered along the way.

The classic metaphor of success is imagining yourself on the winner's platform with the gold medal around your neck, the flag being raised and the national anthem playing.

One of the teams I consulted with in preparation for the 1983 Pan-American Games was under pressure. It had to win a gold medal in order to qualify for the '84 Olympic Games. Funding for their program would be significantly reduced if they didn't make it to the Olympics. So they invested in a sport psychologist to increase their possibilities of success.

I consulted with them for a month in preparation for the games. We worked through a variety of techniques to help the players control the switch on their mental TVs, and to play with more powerful, effective programs. We worked with all aspects of high-performance imagery, especially with mental rehearsal and the use of stimulating images. We defined specific things for each player to do to be at his best (on defense, this might include, "play the transition game, pick up your man/zone, make good reads, play the angles, hustle....")

I created audiotapes for the players highlighting their performance specifics that they could use in conjunction with their mental rehearsal. The tapes also included stimulating images of cats (for quickness, balance, strength) and waves (as a reminder to breathe, and for persistence — "the waves never stop.") Periodically, I would review with each player how his taped imagery sessions were going and do some fine-tuning with them when necessary.

Things went along according to plan except for one team member, named Fred. He had been a world-class player for years, then he became ill. He was diagnosed as having a malignant brain tumor, was operated on and then given a course of radiation treatments and chemotherapy. He was selected to the team and made a cocaptain because of his past excellence and what he had contributed to the team and the sport over the years. And while it was unlikely that he would contribute as a player, it was felt that his presence was a plus, and that he belonged.

I treated Fred much like everyone else. However, his response was unique. Instead of focusing on the elements of mental rehearsal and the specifics of his play, whenever I asked Fred about his imagery he would describe seeing himself standing on the platform after the final game with the gold medal around his neck, the flag being raised and the national anthem being played.

"That's great, Fred," I'd reply, "and I want you to focus on the specific, seeing yourself making the plays, being like a cat." He would agree. Then a few days later when I'd next ask him about his imagery he would reiterate seeing himself standing on a platform with the gold medal being placed around his neck, the flag being raised and the national anthem being played. It went on like that right up to and even through the games. Fred's focus was always the successful end result. Finally, instead of trying to get him to change channels, I simply began to enjoy his image of success.

The team went on to play outstandingly well ... and to win the gold medal. After the final game, I experienced some déjà vu. Standing in the crowd at the base of the awards platform, I looked up at the team and Fred ... and watched them place a gold medal around his neck, saw the flag being raised and heard the national anthem being played.

Later, I acknowledged Fred for his belief and his clear winning focus. He made a difference. Whether it's sport, business or the professions, the ability of the players to believe in and *imagine* their ultimate success is a vital part of winning team play.

On a slightly different mission, an executive responsible for a major trade show described to me that he not only used imagery as a blueprint of what the show would be, but that he'd periodically slip into the future and imagine himself after the show's *successful* completion. In so doing he'd see himself sitting back, feeling relaxed, having a drink at a favorite Chicago restaurant, smoking a cigar and reflecting on a job very well done. He confided that he would frequently tune into that image for sustenance and to keep his energy up during the long, tedious and often frustrating preparatory phase of putting the show together.

I've always believed that it's a lot easier to get up early, in the dark, and go to work or train in the cold and rain if, from time to time, you imagine yourself as the winner you are capable of being and the success you're striving to become. Imagine the fruits of your labors become reality. See them putting the gold medal around your neck. Your creative imagination is boundless.

Imagery has unlimited application in helping people deal with the pressures of life. For example, pain is a great pressure. While running a six-week residential program for people with chronic pain, I discused with the group the three ways I use imagery to enhance performance. Then, I asked them how they could adapt these images to dealing with their chronic pain.

For *mental rehearsal*, they created images of moving and doing everyday things with more ease, greater flexibility and less pain while feeling calm, and with improved posture and biomechanics. Some of the *focal images* they came up with included feeling light and walking with soft cat's feet. Actually, the cat is a wonderful image for people who want to move with more ease and grace. An important part of rehabilitation is having a clear image of something you want to do or be. What we focus on we magnify in our consciousness. If a pain sufferer focuses on pain, the pain becomes magnified and other considerations are peripheral. If a person focuses on what he or she wants to create and on images of success, that gains energy and the pain, though significant, becomes secondary. Some of the *images of success* they imagined included themselves performing and enjoying a variety of activities both vocational (for instance, returning to a previous job, finishing a project they'd started, doing something new and challenging) and recreational (camping with their families, regaining a certain level of fitness and activity). Some imagined themselves acquiring something (buying or building a dream house).

Of course, high-performance imagery is not just about visualizing success. Life is as much about process as result. It's as much about the journey as where you're headed. Rarely, if ever, is it cost-effective to adopt an "at any price" attitude with yourself. Whatever you do, invest your creative imagination in your wellbeing and in experiencing yourself "playing the game" with greater ease and enjoyment. And, if you're one of those people who are locked into succeeding at any price, someone who thinks relaxing is wasteful or detrimental to your performance focus, let me assure you that your ability to imagine and experience yourself playing with more ease, efficiency and grace will not only contribute to some good feeling, it will also result in far more favorable outcomes.

~ Imagination is one of the most powerful qualities of the mind.

~ Imagination is even more powerful than the will.

~ To realize your imagination potential, create a context of success.

~ To do that, release and breathe. Draw in energy.

~ Acknowledge the wonderful person you are.

~ Then, imagine yourself excelling.

~ First, script and define exactly what it is you want to do,
feel and be.

~ Experience yourself "being there," hitting all the elements
perfectly.

~ See yourself like a cat, a rock or a light.

~ Feel yourself confident and at ease.

~ Imagine yourself having achieved your goal.

~ If, from time to time, you experience doubt, distraction, pressure,
stress and dis-ease,

release, breathe and tune into your high-performance imagery.

~ Tune into sensory impressions of yourself at your best.

~ Hold these images.

~ Act on them.

~ Make them real.

~ You control the switch.

CHAPTER 14 TRAINING NOTES

Winning Imagery

1. **Week two:** The first step toward using winning imagery is to actually define the specific elements and the situations that you want to imagine. Script these out and write them down.

2. **During weeks two, three and four,** spend at least four or five *minutes* every day imagining yourself performing with ease, power and effectiveness. First, imagine yourself excelling in relaxed circumstances. Later, under pressure.
It's a good practice to spend a couple of minutes at the start of each day breathing and tuning into some positive, high-performance imagery. *Use the imaging guidelines described in the chapter.*

3. **Throughout the day (during weeks three and four),** run some two- to five-*second* "highlights" of your performing with power and ease. Before undertaking something important, release ... breathe ... and run a winning highlight.

4. Imagine yourself excelling. Remind yourself:
"The mind is like a TV set that watches one program at a time. And I control the switch."
"I enjoy experiencing myself as successful."
"I deserve to express all my ability."

chapter fifteen

SELF-TALK AND POWER THOUGHTS

There are no known limits to human experience.
The only limits are those that you create.

We think 50,000 to 60,000 thoughts a day, thoughts of all kinds. Some thoughts are positive and empowering. However, if you are like most people, approximately two-thirds of your thinking is negative and limiting. Listening to negative and limiting thoughts create negative and limiting memory traces, which can predispose you to more negative and limited thinking.

However, it doesn't have to be that way. If what you're thinking doesn't give you power or pleasure, if you experience yourself dwelling on negatives like, "I can't," "I won't," "I'm not," "you can't," "he/she won't," "don't mess up," or even the somewhat dubious "well, I'll try," the solution is to release, breathe and refocus. Instead of worrying and wondering "what if," think, "I am," or "I can." Focus on possibility.

Joe was an experienced pro quarterback. Following a great start to his seventh pro season, he appeared to lose it. I was called in to work with him after he had thrown a dozen interceptions in his last three games, all of which his team lost. In a situation like that, there's a tendency, even amongst experienced professionals, to think, "Don't throw another interception."

Mind and body are one. Each thought has a feeling component attached to it. A negative thought like, "don't throw another interception" creates a tense feeling (a contraction). The contraction inhibits coordination, timing and concentration, all of which increase the probability of another interception. My job was to assist the quarterback to change channels and bring more ease and a more productive focus to the moment.

We began with breathing and release training. He tuned into the three breathing keys, released tension and began to feel more in control. Then he imagined himself "throwing strikes." He pictured what he called "hitting the blue dots" — putting the ball right on target.

Everyone experiences a negative thought or some doubt from time to time, and pro quarterbacks are no exception. Our game plan was that when Joe experienced any negativity (for example, "don't get intercepted"), he was to use it as a stimulus to change channels, to release, breathe and think "strike."

It was the same off the field. Joe described one instance of a "fan" yelling at him, saying that he was no good and that he was letting the team down. "I know I shouldn't let things like that bother me," he said. "But it did." I told him I understood ... and to be at his best he had to use the negativity, whether it was his or someone else's, as a stimulus for a power thought.

We practiced breathing and release, and he imagined himself throwing strikes. He thought of himself throwing short strikes, deep strikes, flare strikes, post strikes, hook strikes, all shapes and kinds of strikes, in all kinds of circumstances. Throughout, he affirmed that he was the boss, that he controlled the switch and that he threw with ease and pinpoint accuracy.

On the field, Joe also threw strikes. The first weekend following our consultation, he watched the first half of the game from the sideline. Then, he stepped into a losing situation. Relaxed and focused, he threw four touchdown strikes (without an interception). His team won the game and he was selected "player of the week."

We worked together once a week for the rest of the season. In the next three games, Joe threw only one interception and his team won them all. They stopped their slump and went on to the divisional championship. The quarterback played great. He set a club-passing record and expressed both his considerable talent and a remarkable ability to excel under pressure.

POSITIVE THINKING

There are many kinds of "winning thoughts" you can tune into. Most fit into a broad category of success-oriented thinking that we call positive thought.

Successful people often will things to happen. They're positive thinkers who say, "I will" and "I can," and they do. They live a basic rule of thought, which is, you get more of what you think about.

Whether or not you putted well on the last hole ... whether or not you closed the sale ... whether or not you're relating well to the people around you ... release ... breathe ... affirm that you're okay, and focus on the possibility of real-izing your potential, expressing your ability and making your goal a reality.

While shopping one day in a college town in Mississippi, I bumped into a promising rookie on the university golf team. "Dr. Miller," he exclaimed, "I've got it."

"Got what?" I asked.

"From now on, I'm going for it," he replied. "I'm going to focus on the shot I want to make and not the shot I want to avoid. I'm going to tune into the thoughts and feelings I want to experience and not give any power to the ones I don't."

He explained how his new-found positiveness grew out of a real-ization he had while doing some "homework" (mental rehearsal) that I had given the golf team. It had an amazing effect. He drove off with the team to a major collegiate tournament in the southeast and, for the first two rounds, the positive-thinking rookie led the field.

Positive thought is one of the most powerful creative forces at our disposal. It's a force you can consistently put to use to excel under pressure. I usually define with my clients eight to ten "power thoughts" or affirmations. These are positive thoughts that I encourage them to say (and repeat) to themselves for more ease, confidence and impact in any situation, especially under pressure.

Some power thoughts are general. They deal with having more ease, power and control, and they're equally applicable to sport, business, rehabilitation and the arts.

A few examples are:

"I'm the boss."

"I control the switch."

"My mind is a force I use to make things happen."

"I see real clear. I see opportunity everywhere."
"The waves never rush. I deserve my time."
"I deserve to express all my ability."

Some of these thoughts reinforce aspects of imagery and feelings we described earlier as performance enhancing.

"I'm quick and strong as a cat [lion, panther]."
"Energy flows through me like a star."
"I've got a great goal-scoring reflex."
"Some free breathing and a little adrenalin is like a jet fuel."
"I have great hands [touch, eyes …]."
"I have within me the warmth [light] of the sun."
"I'm patient. The waves never rush."
"I am the master of ease."

A plant manager I worked with was a super-high achiever who was extremely successful in "making his numbers." However, he felt he was doing it at considerable expense to himself. While setting his goals for the coming year, he said to me, "I enjoy being successful and I want to continue to be as effective as I've been, but I want to do it with a lot more ease. The affirmation we created for him was, "I am the master of ease." It was perfect. He was a hard-working guy who wasn't ever going to take things too easily. However, the thought and image of being "the master of ease" was a balancing reminder to allow himself more time and to bring a quality of self-respect to his work. Ultimately, it contributed to his having more impact and more joy.

As we said earlier, different personality types are attracted to and respond best to different power thoughts. Task-oriented people respond more to performance-related input, such as: "That's a good job," "I like the way you handled ... [refer to something specific]," "You have excellent ... [again, refer to a specific ability]."

In contrast, the more socially oriented personality responds more to personal validation. "I appreciate you." "You're the kind of person I/we can count on." "You're really an important part of the team."

While most people perform better with self-talk that is supportive and reassuring, some (usually extraverts) stimulate themselves to perform with power thoughts that are demanding and sometimes self-critical.

Whether you're coaching yourself or others, if you like to use challenging thoughts, remember to be consistent. Don't be excessively self-critical or alarming. That only produces contraction.

Self-talk is effective in both the first and second person. (I'm okay," "I can _____" [first person]. "You're okay," "You can _____" [second].) While most people talk to themselves in the first person, we've been conditioned to hearing much of the talk (especially instructions) in the second person. So experiment with how you phrase your self-talk, and find out what empowers you.

Some power thoughts are related to specific tasks and techniques. They support performers by helping them focus on specifics that enhance their game while they are under pressure.

A few power thoughts you might say to yourself while playing tennis include:

"Relax and breathe."

"Racquet back."

"Action balanced."

"Position ready. Shoulder [hips] sideways."

"Feet moving."

"Read the ball [Wilson, Penn.]." ... to improve your focus.

"Bounce ... hit" was something used in the *Inner Game of Tennis* to keep the player focused on the ball during play. Similarly, "stay with the ball" is a power thought to use between points, when the mind is apt to wander to self-criticism, poor officiating or other irrelevancies.

While supervising (one-minute management style), you might say to yourself:

"Define clear, simple goals."

"Provide clear feedback."

"Find something to praise" (task or person).

"Critique the behavior, not the individual."

Earlier in the book, I discussed the case of Stanley, a concert violinist who had a performance problem which resulted in his losing concentration and flow. In Chapter Eight, I described how we worked on developing his "release reflex." Our goal was that Stanley would tighten up and contract but would keep playing whenever he experienced some minor imperfection one inevitably encounters in playing a complex concerto. In addition to the psycho-physical training, we also worked on Stanley's self-talk. As he was a perfectionist who wanted to be in total control, one thought we developed to give him more ease, balance and feeling was, "I play like a gypsy, not an accountant." Stanley enjoyed the thought.

Late one evening after a successful concert in which Stanley had played with a prominent Los Angeles symphony orchestra, I joined a large dinner party. The group consisted of Stanley, his wife, the conductor, relatives of the conductor and the late composer, plus several dignitaries and patrons of the symphony. Late during dinner while discussing Stanley's playing with the daughter-in-law of the composer, I enthusiastically remarked, "He played like a gypsy." Whereupon Stanley, who was seated at the other side of the table, looked up with a smile and said, almost reflexively, "not an accountant."

Some performance thoughts are "love thoughts."
"I love to score."
"I love to hit the ball."
"I love to win."
"I love a challenge."
"I love to sell."
"I love what I sell."
"I love what I contribute."

Actually, "love thoughts" are "super-power thoughts."
Some of the most effective advice I could give to anyone, whether they're stepping up to the plate in a ball game or about to attempt whatever they do in life is, instead of thinking, "I've got to get a hit," or "I've got to _____," release ... breathe ... and think, "I love to hit the ball" or "I love _____."

In any game, just changing the thought "I've got to," which usually denotes a degree of pressure, fear and contraction, into "I love to" can provide a special feeing of ease and power, one that facilitates performance in any situation.

Some power thoughts address a person's feelings about themselves and are intended to build confidence and self-esteem:
"I'm okay,"
"My presence alone is a valuable asset."
"I'm a winner."
"I enjoy winning."

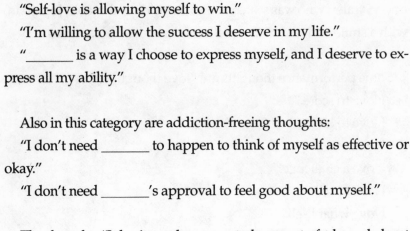

"Self-love is allowing myself to win."

"I'm willing to allow the success I deserve in my life."

"_____ is a way I choose to express myself, and I deserve to express all my ability."

Also in this category are addiction-freeing thoughts:

"I don't need _____ to happen to think of myself as effective or okay."

"I don't need _____'s approval to feel good about myself."

The thought, "I don't need _____ to happen to feel good about myself" is one I use and recommend all the time. Imagine that you are standing in line to get tickets, or at a bank, and someone steps in front of you. There's an immediate emotional response. The intruder is acting as if you are not even there. You start to get angry, to feel uncomfortable. You're not exactly sure what to do. You can feel the pressure building. You're starting to get really pumped. Now you're out of your optimal communication mode. You're ready to explode. If you address that person now, it's going to be with such anger that they'll respond aggressively. The situation could easily turn ugly.

Here's an alternative. Remember, you're the boss. Don't allow yourself to get overly upset and possibly do or say something ineffective and foolish. When you're aware of the pressure ... release it. Take a breath (change channels) and then tune into a power thought like, "I don't need some insensitive/ignorant/or uptight stranger to treat me respectfully in order for me to feel good about myself." Then, somewhat more calmly, tell them to move to the rear of the line.

Mitch was a highly motivated and caring young executive in the steel industry. He was wrestling with a problem with one of the employees he supervised, a man named Gene. "This guy really upsets me," Mitch remarked. "He's careless, slow and sloppy. He's negative. He complains. He challenges everything I say, and I'm not really sure of the best way to deal with him."

I acknowledged Mitch for his desire to do a good job and discussed with him a few things he could do to improve his self-management skills. First, I showed him how to breathe and release for a greater sense of ease and psycho-physical control. Second, I suggested more clarity and structure in programing Gene's time so he would have less to say to the man. Third, I gave Mitch a few power thoughts to work with, including; "I don't need Gene to be respectful [or competent] for me to feel good about myself."

What I wanted Mitch to understand was that Gene didn't upset him, Mitch upset himself. Gene was just expressing his negativity to his new, young boss. In doing so, he was providing Mitch with an opportunity to become a better manager, one that could manage himself. When Mitch saw that, and remembered that he controlled the switch, he began to use Gene's negative behavior to release … breathe … and maintain his positive focus. At that moment, his attitude shifted, the pressure lifted and he actually began to enjoy the challenge.

There's one more interesting thing to note in this example. When Gene realized that Mitch wasn't upsetting himself any more, he let it go out of his negativity and became more productive.

Here are a few coaching suggestions for developing more empowering self-talk.

1. Create eight to ten "power thoughts" that you can rely on to enhance your performance and wellbeing. These are thoughts that will nurture you and that you'll feel good about tuning into when you want a lift.

2. Think positive thoughts. Think thoughts that will inspire and empower you under pressure. The ideal "power thought" is a positive thought that's relevant, that feels good to you, and that's expressed in positive language.

For a skater about to hit a challenging jump thinking, "I'm lightness," "I've got great spring," or "I'm a high-flyer" is preferable and far more uplifting than thinking, "Don't crash."

For a manager making an important decision in the face of uncertainty, thinking, "What I do will be the right decision" or "Everything will work out fine," is preferable and more empowering than thinking a parental, "Don't make a mistake."

For someone selling a service or a product, thoughts like, "We're quality," and, "How can I help you?" are more positive and productive than thinking, "I've got to make this sale," "Got to" is pressure.

For everyone, defining their preferences and thinking of life in terms of "opportunities" and "challenges" is exhilarating and life enhancing. In contrast, being dependant and dwelling on "problems" and "negatives" is exhausting and stressful.

3. Make your power thoughts functional. Keep them brief and relevant. One journalist I consulted with travelled a great deal. He found it much easier to write in his study at home in New England than in hotel rooms and press areas around the globe. Along with some training in psycho-physical control (breathing and release), one affirmation we came up with that he found extremely beneficial (especially when he was attempting to be creative in some strange set-

ting) was, "the world is my workplace." It was also a thought he enjoyed thinking.

For several years, I participated in a goal-setting conference that
one of my corporate clients held each year. The conference is a three-
day retreat during which the management team reviews performance for the previous year and defines and commits to goals for the
year to come. The goals were personal as well as corporate. My job
was to facilitate the managers in defining their goals and then work
with them to create "power thoughts" to support the realization of
these goals.

One manager, the head of product development, was feeling the
push to generate more and better products to support the company's
plans for rapid growth. A few of the power thoughts we came up
with included, "I have a personal connection to an unlimited supply
of good ideas." "I am the leading edge of product innovation in
America today."

He was not immune to criticism and frustration. One day, he was
discouraged and confided, "So many good ideas get shot down
here." To help him deal with the inevitable rejection that surrounded
him and his job, and to be more free and effective, some of the power
thoughts we came up with included:

"I am a free-wheeling, spontaneous, unbounded thinker."

"I enjoy the challenge ... and the pressure."

"I am unaffected by the negative comments of others."

"I am well organized and follow through."

"I communicate and relate well to others."

"We're a winning team. We get the ball across the line."

Whenever I perceive a need and don't do anything about it (whether it's to improve communication, to stop smoking, to lose weight, to cut the grass or to be in better shape), it feels like I create a little more pressure in my life. Some of the power thoughts I've introduced to improve personal lives and lifestyle issues include:

On improving family relations:

"I love and support my family in expressing themselves openly and in achieving their goals."

"There's an abundance of love and warmth for everyone in our family."

On losing weight:

"I'm becoming my ideal weight."

"Everything I eat turns into health and beauty."

What you think about what you eat is a compliment to an intelligent diet and exercise. Thinking, "this is going to make me fat," after you've eaten it, is both nonproductive and stressful. For more on lifestyle see Chapter 18.

On stopping smoking:

"I *can* stop smoking."

"I will look, feel and taste better when I do."

"I enjoy breathing freer and more easily."

On exercise:

"I love to work out."

"I feel, look, work and love better when I'm exercising and in shape."

"Man was made to move, and I'm a quality mover."

4. Create power thoughts you enjoy. Thoughts are the food of your consciousness. Feed your mind positive, powerful, digestible thoughts: thoughts you enjoy thinking. It's your move. You're the director. You're the star. You control the switch.

5. Repeat your power thoughts often. Repetition builds strength. One way to build up the body (for example, the wrists) is to select a simple, effective exercise (curls) and do a lot of repetitions. One way to develop some thought power is to define a few clear, empowering affirmations and do lots of repetitions with them.

You can memorize and repeat these power thoughts to yourself. You can put them on tape and listen to them at various times during the day. Or you can write them down. What's important is that you develop the response of saying something facilitative to yourself when you're under pressure.

For example, if you're someone who's stressed by rushing all the time, an appropriate thought might be, "The waves never rush."

~ As you write that affirmation, release and breathe.
~ As you breathe, give yourself time for the inbreath to come all the way in.
~ Give yourself time for the outbreath to go all the way out. You deserve your time.
~ Write down your affirmation a number of times (100-200 times). If you find yourself impatient, rushing and stressing yourself too much of the time, take a breath or two and write, "The waves never rush. The waves never rush. The waves never rush. The waves never rush."

~ As you write, other thoughts will come to mind. They may be irrelevant distractions (thinking about what you had for dinner) or negative thoughts (thinking that what you're writing is nonsense, that it doesn't make a difference, or that you've got to rush to get ahead).

~ Notice these thoughts. Don't argue with yourself. Simply release ... breathe ... and refocus. Go back to writing your power thought.

~ Rewrite (rethink), "The waves never rush."

~ Gradually, that thought will become stronger, and you will experience yourself rushing less.

6. Combine your power thoughts with breathing and release. This is fundamental.

We are psycho-physical beings. Working with thought, breath and release is an ideal combination to maximize performance and wellbeing. The limitation of many positive thought programs is that they aren't psycho-physical. They don't integrate mind and matter.

It's difficult and limiting to think positively when you're tense, angry or depressed. It's far more effective to release, breathe and then focus on the positive. The converse is also true. Release without direction can lead to confusion and collapse.

Release, breathe and think power thoughts.

One of my clients, an aggressive and talented young hockey player, was struggling to make the Edmonton Oilers, a perennial NHL championship team in the mid-eighties. Shortly after he got to training camp, he developed a serious case of "making the team anxiety." Instead of keeping his focus on what was happening on the ice, he found himself tuning into the coach's experience. He kept asking himself, "Did he notice me do this? ... Do that? ... Why did (didn't) he play me on that line? ... What's he thinking?"

His desire to excel and impress was understandable. However, cueing the coach instead of tuning into feelings of power, ease and competence caused tension and poor concentration and limited his play. He was sent down to the minor leagues.

The following year, he was again invited to camp. He sought me out for something that would help him to stay loose and focused. He knew that he was a better player than he had shown them the previous year, and he wanted to play to his potential. (He also had some anger and some thoughts that he hadn't been treated fairly by the organization.)

The program we developed encouraged him to loosen up, tune into his breathing, inspire himself, feel powerful, then think "I belong" ... and experience himself playing well.

That year at camp, he played well and he had a good time. Every time he'd think about the coach and start to wonder, "What's he thinking?" or, "He/they didn't give me a chance," he'd use that limiting thought as a reminder (a stimulus) to change channels, to release ... breathe ... and refocus. He would tune into his winning program. He'd think thoughts like, "I'm the boss." "I control the switch." "I've got a great goal-scoring reflex." "I'm quick and strong as a cat." And "I love to score goals." And, he'd imagine himself taking a pass or stealing the puck and shooting it into the net.

The moment he stopped focusing on his attachment to making the team and tuned into the process of "being there" and playing the game of hockey effectively, he stopped interfering with himself. He played better, and had more fun doing it. That year, he started the season with the NHL club. Five years later, he was still playing in the league.

The very same pressure to impress and "make it" that the young hockey player encountered is shared by aspirants in all high-performance fields from sport to sales. Whatever your situation, whatever you're attempting to do, remember to release, breathe, focus on the positive. Empower yourself with winning thoughts.
Think "I am ..." "I can ..." or "I belong ..." You get more of what you think about.

Probably the most positive thing about being a pessimist is that you're rarely disappointed.

CHAPTER 15 TRAINING NOTES

Self-talk and Power Thoughts

1. **Week one**: Give some constructive thought to your self-talk.
    Define eight to ten "power thoughts" (no more than ten).
    Write them down.
    Memorize them.
    Repeat them to yourself at least two or three times a day.
    Remember, repetitions build strength.

2. **During weeks two, three and four:** Review your thought list
    each week. Eliminate or edit those thoughts that don't give
    you power. Add at least one new thought each week that you
    find stimulating and empowering. Eliminate those that are
    not productive or appealing. Write your power thoughts
    down (100 times).
    Memorize them.
    Repeat them to yourself several times a day.

3. Put your power thoughts on a cassette recorder. Listen to
    them throughout your day, whenever you have a free ear
    (when driving a car).

4. Having a clear, empowering self-talk can be a source of
    strength and a positive focus under pressure. Remember:

    **"Creative thought is one of the most powerful forces on the
    planet."**
    "I get more of what I think about."
    "I think power thoughts."
    "Repetition builds strength."

chapter sixteen

FEELINGS OF COMPETENCE AND CONFIDENCE

*When I'm feeling really stressed and burned out, the
kids had better watch it. Something they do that I might
have smiled at a few hours earlier can trigger a biting,
destructive remark from me. Half the time I don't even
realize it's happening until it's simply too late.*
~ A parent

Feelings are basic. In the course of a day, we can experience the whole range of emotions from happiness, joy, confidence and calm to sadness, frustration, anger, insecurity, fear and fatigue. Much of the time, we're not aware of or in control of our feelings. Yet our feelings color our perception, and shape our thoughts and images.

Under pressure, the feeling that usually dominates is fear, with both motivating and anxiety-producing qualities.

One of the keys to consistent high-level performance is your ability to use your mind to create the feelings that empower you. In this chapter, we're going to look at four different types of feelings that you can create that will enhance your ability to perform under pressure.

They are:

1. **Feeling Good;**
2. **Feelings of Competence;**
3. **Feeling Confident;**
4. **A Sense of Deserving.**

FEELING GOOD is basic to health and consistent high-level performance. Good feelings involve some of the same breathing and release feelings that we've been discussing throughout the book.

They're *feelings of rhythm and time.* Tune into your breathing rhythm. Give yourself time for the inbreath to become an outbreath. You'll feel better and operate with more wisdom and power by giving yourself more time.

They're *feelings of energy and continuity.* Inspire yourself. Feel yourself breathing in energy. Feel your personal connection to an unlimited supply of energy. Connect the inbreath to the outbreath, the outbreath to the inbreath. The waves never stop. They can wash anything away. That force is with you.

It's *the feeling of being in the moment.* Worry resides in the past and the future. Move into the present. Experience the point where the inbreath becomes an outbreath. The power is in the moment.

It's *the feeling of releasing* excessive tension, stress and worry. Tension is dis-ease. It limits performance and wellbeing. Release, breathe and feel energy streaming to you.

Release and breathe. *Experience feelings of power and ease.* Loving yourself is allowing yourself to shine. Remember, you deserve to feel good. And you deserve to express all your ability.

Imagine being in a crowded room. Many people are talking to you and at you. In one way or another, they all seem to be asking more of you. They want more of your attention, more of your time, more of your money or more of your affection. They want you to be more careful, more productive or more successful. They're pushing you to make more of an impression and more of a difference, especially when it counts. In effect, they are reinforcing your very own feelings. For some time, you've been pressuring yourself to be and do more. The room feels like an uncomfortable, pressing place. You wish you could escape.

Suddenly, you notice a small door in the wall. You open it and step into another room, one that's peaceful. It's a quiet place, colored in soft, pastel shades. Instantly, you feel more calm and comfortable. This place reminds you of the peacefulness you've experienced as a child in your room or at times in the country. After a few minutes in the quiet, you notice yourself thinking, "Is there something else, more important, I should be doing right now?" As this thought comes to mind, you feel an uneasiness stir within you. You hear a sound. You look up and notice a large TV screen in the room. On the screen is your thought, "Is there something else, more important, that I should be doing now?" You see yourself feeling uneasy.

For a moment, you are distracted by the experience of watching yourself. Then you recall some unfinished business. There's something you didn't do that you feel you should have handled. On the screen, you're now experiencing that thought, and the pressure and uneasiness associated with it. You begin to wonder if you are okay. Here you are, in a quiet, peaceful space, and you're upsetting yourself again. You ask yourself, "What's wrong with me?" And as you do, you observe the thought "What's wrong with me?" appear on the TV screen along with the feeling of dis-ease that goes with it.

All of a sudden, you are aware that this is your TV, and that you can control the switch and change the feeling. You remember to release tension and tune into your breathing. You slip into your breathing rhythm. You give yourself more time. You draw in energy. You inspire yourself. You let the tension and noise fall away. You refocus. In just a moment, the room feels comfortable again. You feel more calm and centered. You enjoy that feeling. You remind yourself that you deserve to feel good. You deserve to express your ability. And you control the switch.

Imagine now that you open the door and move back into the crowded, noisy room of endless demands and pressures. Only this time you remember to release and breathe and to stay with feelings that empower you. You feel calm and centered. You get on with your mission ... and you perform well.

> *Nothing external to me can have any power over me.*
> *~ Walt Whitman*

In neurolinguistic programing (nlp), there's a process called *anchoring* that is sometimes used to help people perform in a variety of stressful and high-pressure situations. What it involves is remembering positive feelings you've had associated with doing something well. For example, you might recall specific feelings of competence and confidence you experienced after successfully completing a certain project or achieving an important goal. When you have clear recall of these feelings, you're instructed to do something physical, like "squeeze your thumb." You may be instructed to repeat that process several times and/or to recall another empowering feeling memory and squeeze the thumb again.

The idea is that pairing a powerful positive feeling with a simple physical response like thumb squeezing will connect the two. With repetitions, the connection is strengthened and the empowering feelings are anchored and accessible. Thereafter, whenever you are in stressful circumstances, simply making the simple physical response will bring to consciousness the empowering feelings you've anchored and help you to perform under pressure.

In my experience, pairing powerful memories with taking a breath is the most effective way to anchor your performance-enhancing feelings.

Jim Beattie was a fine pitcher with the Seattle Mariners, the ace of the staff. The two years we worked together, 1983 and 1984, were two of his best. One day, I was watching him pitch against the Oakland A's, and he was doing great. He had a perfect game through six innings. In the top of the seventh, Oakland's leadoff batter, Ricky Henderson, hit a single ... and something shifted.

Now the hit itself wasn't important. A double play erased the runner. However, something changed. Instead of pitching with a smooth rhythm and an apparent ease, Jim began to take more time.

He looked less comfortable, more nervous and fidgety. His pitch se-lection also changed. Instead of going at the hitters, he started to throw more breaking balls and pitch around them. He survived the seventh inning still leading 1-0. But then in the eighth, he lost it. The A's scored a bunch of runs, and Jim was taken out of the game, which the A's ultimately won.

I met with Jim two days later and asked him about the perfor-mance.

"Did anything change for you after that hit in the seventh?"

"Not really," he replied. "Some people said I changed my pitch selection and threw more breaking balls, but I don't think I did."

Then I asked him if he had changed his thinking in any way after the hit.

He thought about it, then he said, "Well, maybe I did. Before the hit I was into it. I was feeling really good. I was just relaxed and throwing strikes. After the hit, I guess I tightened up a little and I be-gan to think, *'There's only nine outs to go.'*"

It was when Jim changed his focus from being in the present (from this breath, this pitch) to worrying about the future (there's only nine outs to go) that he slipped out of the moment, out of the groove, lost his edge, and lost the game.

We all slip out of the groove from time to time. It's often the same push to excel, and the same fear of failure that causes us to tense, work and stress too much. If this happens to you, if you find yourself pressing, squeezing too hard and worrying "What will happen if," then simplify things. Release and breathe. Focus on feelings of ease and power. Bring those feelings to your performance. You control the switch.

Two ways to strengthen feelings of power and ease and the attitude that goes along with them are: 1. repeatedly be aware of releasing tension and breathing easily throughout the day, and 2. take a short "power break," five to ten minutes of tuning into your breathing, releasing, streaming and focusing on a calming, empowering stimulus. I usually recommend that my clients take a brief "power break" every day during their season. In sport, the season can last six to eight months. In business, it can be all year long.

The "release reflex" and the "power break" are two ways to nurture and reinforce winning feelings and to enhance performance. *They work together.* The more you experience and work with the longer process, the better able you'll be to use the "release reflex" to change channels under pressure — and in an instant. Either way, release … breathe … and focus on feelings of power and ease.

Remember, your motivation to succeed and your commitment to excel energize you. That drive can either give you an edge, or it can stimulate you to push and squeeze too hard and be limiting. In Chapter Two, I described a Dodger pitcher in a "slump." He was a well-motivated, intelligent professional with ten years' experience in the major leagues, yet after a string of unsuccessful appearances he really began to feel the pressure, and he was not reacting well to it. One of the things that helped him to regain his confidence and composure was refocusing on feelings of ease and power. It provided a focus of something other than what could go wrong. And his performance improved dramatically.

To insulate yourself from the limiting, stressful properties of pressure, invest a little time every day tuning into feelings of power and ease. After all, you deserve to feel good. And you deserve to express all of your ability.

FEELINGS OF COMPETENCE. A second kind of winning feelings to tune into are those that are associated with certain aspects of high performance. These are feelings generated by left brain "how to" strategies and the specific things we feel and do when we're performing well.

For the golfer, it may be having "soft hands," a slow, smooth backswing, the feeling of keeping his/her head on the ball, and the feel of striking down and through the ball. The most common golf error is pulling the head off the ball usually to see where it is going. It happens because people want to do well and they interfere with the complete experience of stroking through the ball. Their desire to control the future interferes with their experience and feelings of the present.

For a counselor or a negotiator, a feeling of competence may be patience, calmness, clarity and resolve while being open to where the other person is coming from.

For the dentist, a feeling of competence is working in a relaxed, methodical way from start to finish, step by step, not rushing, in control, feeling no matter what presents itself you can handle it painlessly and easily. It's having a special rapport, both with the patient and the assistant.

For the salesperson, it's feeling energetic, informed, directed, caring, positive — with lots of self-esteem. Self-esteem is the most important factor in the success of a salesperson.

Of course, there's no "right feeling" of high-level performance that applies to everyone. Feelings of competence vary for each of us according to our make-up, history, style, sensitivity and role. What's important is that you become increasingly aware of the feelings you want to create, the feelings that work for you. And that you become more effective at creating them.

Mark Jerue was a Ram linebacker, a special teams captain and a super-intense competitor. The first season, we worked together on breathing and release techniques and mental rehearsal. The next year, he became a starter and wanted something to pace himself and keep him from getting too intense. (Mark had a history of getting so intense that he'd cramp.) He specifically wanted to have more control of his feelings so that he could use his energy more efficiently, think more clearly and to be able to react at his best, play after play.

We developed a special "A, B, C, D, E, F, G, H" program for Mark. Between every play, Mark would think, "A, B, C, D, E, F, G, H." A, B, C mean A = always, B = breathe and C = calm. As soon as the play was over, Mark would think ABC, take a few breaths and calm down. Then, a little more at ease (and having the judgment that brings) he'd think D, E, F, G. D meant down and distance (second and two, or third and eight). E meant evaluate (Mark would review the probabilities of what the opposition was likely to do in that situation). F referred to formation (two wide receivers right, two tight ends in, wide receiver left). Each formation cued Mark to specific responsibilities. Then Mark would think G, for guard. He'd read the guard for pass and run possibilities. Lastly, Mark would think H for hit, which meant intensify feelings and be ready for war.

The program worked extremely well. It was simple enough to remember even under the intense emotion of the game, and it gave Mark the ability to regulate his feelings. Mark had an excellent season that year. For the first fifteen games of the season, he led the team in tackles.

In 1983, I worked with three sprinters at the Pan-American Games in Caracas. The three had flown to Venezuela directly from Finland, where they had competed in the World Championships. Not only had they performed poorly but there was some emotional upset between the three athletes and one of their teammates. They were scheduled to compete three and four days later, and their prospects were not very good. The team manager asked me to work with them.

When I first met them, they looked tense and tired and they described themselves accordingly. Of course, that's not a feeling state likely to produce success.

I began by showing them how to ease up. We spent an hour releasing and breathing ... and they relaxed. The next day we spent a little more time relaxing, creating positive feelings and then pairing those feelings with thoughts like, "I deserve to feel good" and "I control the switch." At our third meeting, the next day the athletes were noticeably more at ease. As they did more relaxation and breathing, I combined the good feeling with thoughts like, "I deserve to feel good" and "I deserve to express my ability." Then we began what I call "constructive wondering."

I asked the three women how fast could a woman run the 400 meters. "Think about it," I said. "If a healthy young woman with all the right physical attributes was wisely trained in her formative years, very well coached, in great shape and everything was just right for her ... just how fast could she run the 400 meters?" It was a positive question. One that reinforced their shift in focus from limitation to possibility. The time they estimated was almost fifteen seconds faster than the world record.

Next, I said, "I know you're all little tired ... but let's say you wake up tomorrow feeling fine ... loose and strong. And let's say you ran a great race. Just how good could you be tomorrow?" They smiled and laughed. All of them responded with a time that was better than their personal best.

In the next two days, they all went out and ran great races. One won a gold medal and set a Pan-American record in the 400 meters. All three won silver medals in the 4x100 meter replay. One ran a personal best.

Breathing and release … plus some creative positive thinking are basic ingredients in developing feelings of competence.

FEELINGS OF CONFIDENCE. Confidence literally means "with faith." It's a feeling that "I'm okay," "I can" and "I will" that often comes from having done it before, and having done it well. If you haven't had that experience, if you haven't done it or if you haven't been doing it consistently well, one way to strengthen confidence is to combine feelings of ease, power, deservedness and competence with winning thoughts and high-performance images.

Luke was a scorer and an NHL All-Star. When he was a star, he went to the net with a definite confidence and the sense that he could make the play. If he didn't have the puck, he played as if it would be there for him. When he had the puck on his stick and he was in front of the net, he felt sure he could beat the goalie and score. He didn't think about it, he knew it. I met him several years later, after he had experienced a few injuries and been traded a number of times. He no longer had "the feeling." He didn't burst to the net anymore. He didn't expect the pass in front. He was no longer sure he'd beat the goalie and score. He lacked confidence and his play was routine and uninspired.

He was motivated and intelligent, and he could still skate like the wind, so we began to work at rebuilding his self-image. The first thing I did was to teach/remind him to release and breathe. I encouraged him to take a "power break" and do fifteen minutes of breathing every day. As he relaxed, he felt good. He felt free from the pressure and fear that surrounded him. I reminded him that the feeling of ease was natural, that he deserved to feel good and that he was okay.

As Luke relaxed and lightened up, he was able to imagine himself playing great hockey. First, he would imagine himself going to the net, taking a pass, shooting accurately and scoring. Then he'd see himself going to the net, drawing the defenseman and making a sharp, accurate pass. He'd imagine himself executing perfectly, with speed and ease. And he'd do a lot of repetitions. He'd imagine the same plays again and again. Between each scene, he'd release and breathe, then he'd imagine the play again. Gradually, we expanded the repertoire of plays he'd mentally rehearse to include more complexity, and playing under more pressure. He'd release, breathe, create some winning feelings and then imagine himself making all the plays — and playing great.

We also looked at defining his role. His fear got him into fights that he didn't belong in. Fighting was an inappropriate preoccupation. He was a goal scorer and a skater, not a policeman. He got that it was essential for him to play his game 100 percent. When he was provoked, he was to use the experience, not to retaliate thoughtlessly or automatically but to "change channels," release ... breathe ... and refocus on creating chances.

We met every ten days for about three months. Sessions lasted about an hour. Luke was encouraged to spend some time each day doing his homework (breathing, releasing, imagining, thinking and feeling effective). Gradually, the feelings, the focus and the self-image became stronger. So did his confidence and his attitude about himself. He wasn't the same player he had been years before — but then, who ever is? In the old days, he did things instinctively, without thinking about them. Now he used his mind more assertively to create the feelings of power, ease and competence that lifted his game. Bottom line, the faith was back. He regained his confidence, he was having more fun and he was playing well.

Julie was having a "confidence problem." She was especially uptight about a presentation on exercise and diabetes she was going to make to a group of physicians at the hospital with which she was associated. Julie's fears were quite unreasonable when you consider that she knew her topic very well. She spent hours every day exercising and leading exercise groups. She had considerable experience counseling people, including diabetics, about the benefits of exercise. And she had spent months researching the subject. I asked her what about the upcoming presentation worried her.

"Is it that you're not prepared?"

"No," she replied.

"Do you think they may be more knowledgeable than you about the subject?"

"No."

"Do you think they're likely to harass or embarrass you?"

"No."

"Then what is it?" I asked.

What Julie eventually came up with had to do with her not feeling good about herself. She was concerned that in the pressure of the moment, and in front of what she perceived to be a prestigious authority group, she might do something to reveal some part of herself that wasn't okay.

I began by helping her to relax and breathe, to feel good. As with the hockey player, we reinforced the notion that she deserved to feel good, that feeling good was natural and that she controlled the switch. Julie practiced releasing, breathing and feeling good. When she could really feel this, she began to imagine herself talking about her experience. I reminded her that she was the absolute and ultimate expert on her experience of exercise. She imagined herself describing the benefits of exercise that she experienced and how it contributed to her feeling better. Then she imagined talking about some of the people she counseled, including those with blood sugar problems who felt better on the exercise programs she prescribed. She added to her experience some of the research findings she had read about.

Julie felt comfortable and confident talking about experiences she had working with others. She relaxed and did some mental rehearsal running through her presentation in her imagination ... and being very well received by the group. To cover any eventuality, I asked her to imagine the audience as being critical, unpleasant and disagreeing with her. While this would have been quite threatening earlier, she now found the possibility amusing ... and unlikely. Even under these circumstances Julie could imagine herself as calm, breathing, and then as before sharing her expertise and knowledge. She rehearsed this several times.

Julie's presentation was extremely successful. She confronted her fear and she emerged from the experience feeling better about herself ... and with the technology to strengthen feelings of confidence should the need arise.

Marie was an Edie Piaf-style singer who believed that "feelings" were the message she wanted to communicate in her songs. She especially enjoyed singing in a small cabaret-type clubs in southern California where she felt the atmosphere was more personal and intimate. When I asked her what feelings she wanted to experience when she sang, her response was both audience-oriented and contradictory. She said "It's strange. I want the audience to love me ... and yet, I want to feel as if they're not even there."

It was Marie's fear and lack of confidence that caused her to focus on the audience's feelings instead of her own. She understood that. The question was, what could she do about it?

Working with the breathing and release techniques, I showed her that the power was with her ... the power was in rhythm ... and the power was in the moment. As Marie began to shift her focus to feeling more ease and power, we then had her address the specific feeling element that she wanted to project in the song.

After two sessions, Marie was able to refocus. Like many people who are unsure of themselves, she was unwilling to acknowledge the role others played in helping her. "What you're saying is great," she said. "But it's nothing I didn't already know. It's just that under pressure I don't think about my feelings."

"Most people don't," I replied. "Now you know what to do about it. Whenever you experience yourself worrying about 'them' ... and what **they're** thinking or feeling, remember the power is with **you**. You're the boss. You deserve to feel good ... and to express all your ability. Then allow yourself to draw in some of that unlimited energy that's all around you and let it flow to you in your song." With a few more sessions she was able to do that more easily.

Performing Under Pressure is about winning feelings. It's about experiencing feelings of power and ease instead of tension and disease. It's about creating a context for generating positive, productive thoughts and images instead of worry, limitation and doubt. It's about feeling confident, focused and in the moment. For the hockey player, it was feeling, thinking and playing like, "I love to score goals," and "I make it happen." For the exercise physiologist, it was letting go of her dis-ease and validating herself as a person and an expert whose experience was unique and meaningful. For the singer, opening up to her feelings and allowing her to express her power and beauty.

DESERVING. When it comes to success, plain and simple, some people feel they deserve it, and some don't.

Wayne was a struggling insurance salesman. He took a "Money Seminar" to develop his prosperity consciousness. Part of the training involved learning a list of prosperity affirmations, including, "I deserve large amounts of money," Wayne said he enjoyed using some of the affirmations; however, he noticed that whenever he said to himself, "I deserve large amounts of money," he felt uneasy. For some reason, he confided, it just didn't feel right to him to be thinking like that. As Wayne and I explored these feelings, he became aware that some of the thoughts and feelings he had about himself were blocking his success.

Instead of spending months talking with Wayne about past conditioning and how his upbringing may have contributed to his lack of self-esteem, we worked directly with changing Wayne's *feelings of deserving*.

We began by having Wayne tune into his breathing and relax deeply. As he gave himself time to draw in energy and let it stream through his body, he began to feel good. Then I had him acknowledge that he *deserved* to feel good ... and that it was natural to feel that way. Wayne readily agreed. He could actually feel it. Then I asked him to imagine himself excelling at something. At first, he chose to imagine himself communicating easily and effectively with his clients ... and enjoying the situation. I reminded Wayne that he deserved to express his ability, all his ability. Then, as he continued to relax and breathe, I asked him to imagine himself with a great deal of money. "How would you express yourself — what would you do with lots of money?" Again, I reminded Wayne that he deserved to express all his ability. He came up with a number of pleasant ways to spend and enjoy money.

I asked Wayne to create images to go with thoughts like, "I deserve to express myself with money," and "I create health, happiness and joy with my money." As Wayne experienced these phrases, I made it clear to him that no one was suggesting that he needed money, that he deserved to have to more than somebody else or that he should do anything to get it. We were simply providing him with an opportunity to open himself to the possibility of creating, receiving and of being able to express himself with money.

That interplay of breath, feeling and thought is very powerful. In just four sessions plus some homework (repetitions build strength), Wayne experienced a significant shift in his feelings, enough to enjoy the feeling that went with the thought, "I deserve large amounts of money."

For some people, money is a mirror. In Wayne's case, the shift he experienced in his feelings about money was a reflection of him taking a step toward greater self-appreciation and toward realizing more of who he was and what was possible.

Cliff was another "deserving" example. He was a good collegiate tennis player who played numbers four and five on the MSU tennis team. I was asked to work with him when his coach observed that he almost never won the first set. The coach also noted that once Cliff fell behind he would play much better. However, the problem was that Cliff simply wasn't a good enough tennis player to go around spotting his opponents the first set.

When I heard that he started poorly, my first thought was that Cliff probably was too tight going into the match. As I've said throughout the book, the pressure to excel at everything from playing tennis and pitching baseballs to selling product, making love and speaking effectively causes people to tense up and contract. So, I began by addressing the tension and working with Cliff's ability to release and breath.

After a short time, it was apparent that precompetition tension wasn't Cliff's problem. The issue was that Cliff simply didn't believe he deserved to win. What made matters more interesting was that Cliff was also clear he didn't deserve to lose. The result was that whenever he was down he'd become more aggressive and play with abandon and impact. What we all wanted Cliff to do was to bring his competitive spirit and drive to his play from the *beginning* of the match.

Again, I chose not to work in depth with his questionable self-esteem. Instead, he got into his breathing and relaxed deeply. He acknowledged that he deserved to feel good, and that it was natural. Then I asked him to imagine himself playing well. As he did, he repeated the thought, "I deserve to express my ability ... all my ability." I explained to Cliff that the match was not about him versus some other guy; it was not about who was better. It was about him playing himself. The other guy was simply there to provide him with the opportunity to express his outstanding ability (his gift). And *he deserved to express it.*

Cliff was able to create the bridge from feeling good and acknowledging that he deserved it to seeing himself excelling and feeling that he deserved to express his ability. Once he could do that, he never had another problem with the first set. Of course, he may sometimes have lost to better players, but his play was consistent.

A key to shifting mindset is to go back to the basics — to breathing and release, to feelings of power, ease and a sense of deserving ... and then refocusing and addressing the situation.

~ Excellence is a very personal affair.
~ Examine your performance feelings.
~ Take inventory.
~ Define the specific feeling elements that go with your performing well.
~ Think about both the feelings you want to experience more of ... and less of.
~ Be aware of how, when and where you feel pressure ... and how you can effectively deal with it.

~ Use your mind assertively to create the feelings you want.
~ Release ... breathe ... and focus on feelings of power, ease and competence.
~ Remember, your feelings create your thoughts and images.
~ You deserve to express your ability.
~ You control the switch.

CHAPTER 16 TRAINING NOTES

Winning Feelings

1. **Week one:** Practice breathing and releasing.

2. **Week two:** Take inventory. Define the kinds of feelings that you want to recreate in your life, feelings of ease, power, competence and confidence.

   Recall the exact circumstance when you felt each of these feelings. Recall where you were, what you were wearing, what you were doing or did, and most importantly, how you felt at the time.

   Create a feeling script. Write down those feelings. Be specific. Develop as clear a blueprint as possible of feelings you want to create.

   Throughout the process, remember to release and breathe. Releasing and breathing improves the quality of your feeling memory and it enables you to recreate those feelings more easily. After you have created a power feeling, take a breath and connect that simple action of breathing to empowering yourself.

3. **Weeks three and four:** Every morning on awakening, spend a moment releasing and breathing and creating an empowering feeling for the day. Half a dozen times a day, take a breath and recreate that feeling.

chapter seventeen

A WINNING
ATTITUDE

Attitude is a matter of choice.
~ Lee Thomas

The winning team in sport and in business is not necessarily the one with the biggest, strongest players or the greatest assets. Rather, it's the team that is best able to stimulate and channel the energy of the individuals and the group toward success. It's the team with a winning attitude.

The three things to keep in mind about attitude are:

1. **Your attitudes color your perceptions and affect your beliefs and actions.**

2. **Your attitudes are your own. You create them.**

3. **Attitudes can be changed.**

An attitude is a predisposition to respond. It's a consistent way of behaving that makes it more or less likely that certain things will happen. A high-stress attitude is a behavior pattern that predisposes us to stress and dis-ease. A winning attitude is a way of thinking, feeling and acting that predisposes us to success.

Sport, like all competition, provides an excellent forum for demonstrating the impact of a positive or winning attitude ... and the scouts know this. In baseball, when scouting a young prospect, an organization looks at both physical and mental qualities in determining who will be a big leaguer.

When I worked with the New York Mets organization, they would review each player every year for physical and skill dimensions like speed, strength, hitting, fielding and throwing. And they would discuss "make-up." Make-up is a baseball term that incorporates how motivated the individual is. How do they respond to coaching? Do they have composure? What's their ability to perform under pressure? There are innumerable examples of players with seemingly limited physical skills passed over in selection drafts who went on to become stars because of a winning attitude and their willingness to persevere and do whatever was necessary to get the job done.

In football, make-up is often called "character," and it's given top priority in selecting talent. In the mid-seventies, when the Dallas Cowboys were "America's Team," one thing they did to ensure that they would be recruiting the best available talent was to hire a psychologist to help them assess the character of prospective draftees. Their thinking was, and still is, that the right attitude is as important to success as physical skill. Indeed, at the highest levels of performance, estimates about the contribution of the mental component to success vary from fifty to ninety percent.

Four qualities that I associate with a consistent high-performance attitude are motivation, commitment, mental toughness and love.

1. Motivation: In healthy people, there is a natural desire to excel. Paradoxically, it's that very same desire that creates pressure. The principal emotion that limits motivation and performance is *fear*. People fear many things. Some fear failure and what it might say about them. They think of doing as "being" and interpret not doing or not succeeding as a statement that they are not okay. To protect themselves from fear and the pain of embarrassment, some people unconsciously suppress their desire to excel, and become negative. After all, if you don't think you can or you will, you won't be surprised and disappointed if you don't.

This pattern sometimes shows up in teams that lose repeatedly. I've seen professional athletes on losing teams get very upset with each loss … for a while. Then some players begin to adapt to failure and develop a losing attitude characterized by thinking like, "Well, it's not *my* fault. I did my job." Or, "What's the use?" Of course, they still have to play, so they go through the motions of performing game after game, but they do it without the emotion and enthusiasm that can really make a difference. People subjected to repeated losses may or may not be aware of what's happening to them, but they often become defensive. It hurts to give 100 percent and not succeed. As one player said, "A part of me dies when I lose."

In almost every endeavor, there are people who would prefer to avoid the pain and embarrassment of going for something, not achieving it and looking foolish. They become professional losers and respond to challenge and pressure by withdrawing their spirit. They forget that we lose more, and more often, by not investing ourselves.

People with a winning attitude want to excel. They don't focus on what will happen if they are not successful. Instead, they see a challenge as an opportunity to express their talent.

Four ways to strengthen your motivation are:

Improve your health. As I said earlier, healthy people possess a natural desire to excel. As you improve your health (see Chapter 18), you will also increase your desire and the confidence to express yourself.

*Improve the quality of your **mental** diet.* Specifically, improve what you say to yourself and what you imagine. Expose yourself to people and experiences that empower and lift you (that includes your self-talk and imagery). Regularly, imagine yourself experiencing and being whatever it is you really want to do and be. Stay tuned into the empowerment channel.

Make a want list. Wants are different from goals. Getting in touch with your wants supplies you with a wellspring of energy that can be channeled into meaningful goals. Every two or three months, write down at least twenty-five things you want to accomplish, experience or have: health wants (to lose weight, increase activity levels, stop smoking); relationship wants (to develop a new and meaningful relationship, improve relationship with mate, parent or children); career wants (a successfully completed project, career change, a more interesting job, greater responsibility, better pay); material wants (a new car, house, clothes, money); recreational wants (to run a marathon, reduce your golf handicap, learn to play a musical instrument, or how to speak French); spiritual wants (personal contentment, peace on earth).

Create clear, meaningful goals. Choose one goal from each group on your "want list" (health, relationship, career, material, recreational, spiritual). Select a goal you genuinely *want* to invest your energy in. Something that's really meaningful to you. The difference between a want and a goal is the willingness to invest your energy into making the goal a reality. I can say, "I want world peace," or "I want to make the Olympic team, or to lead the company in sales." However, unless I'm actually going to give that want a priority in my life, make a commitment to investing my energy, time and spirit in it, and commit myself to making it happen, it will just be a want, and not a goal. Be explicit. Define:

What your goal is _____

Who's going to do it? _____

By when? _____

Where? _____

How much? _____

For example, if you were obese and wanted to set a health goal to lose weight:

Define what the goal is.	*To lose weight.*
Who's going to do it?	*I am.*
By when? Specify the date.	*January 1, 199__.*
Where? Specify where you'll be.	*Vancouver, Los Angeles.*
How much weight you will lose.	*Twenty pounds.*

Develop an action plan to realize your goal. Decide on a strategy. Lay out a clear, step-by-step action plan or blueprint that will help you to achieve your goal. The plan is a guideline. It's not etched in stone. It's there to assist you, not to create pressure.

Mike is the sales manager for one of Canada's largest insurance companies. He called to ask if I was available to talk to his branch office. As we spoke, he related an interesting story. Mike said that just after taking his new job he was reviewing a list of goals he had set when I had consulted with his sales team eighteen months earlier. He was impressed by the fact that many of the things he listed as goals had become a reality in a short time.

A corporate career goal he had set was that his sales team would lead the company in monthly sales volume. They were twentieth the month we began working together. In March of 1991, his last month with that sales team, they were number one in the sales for the entire company. A personal career goal Mike set was that he be appointed sales manager of one of two specific branch offices in British Columbia. "Two months ago," he said, "I was appointed sales manager of one of those offices." A material goal Mike set for himself was to own a forty-foot boat. Eighteen months later, he was the proud owner of a thirty-seven-foot boat.

"It's amazing what can happen when you get clear about what you want … and are willing to commit to it," declared Mike, "I'd like the people in the branch to experience the process."

Having clear, meaningful goals to focus on, a graduated plan for their realization, and regular, positive self-acknowledgment is a powerful insulation against the stresses of life and an enormous step toward getting what you want.

2. Commitment: Commitment flows from desire and to a goal. Until you are actually committed, there is a hesitancy, an uncertainty, a tendency to hold back and give less than 100 percent. Commitment is both the decision to go for it and the willingness to do whatever is necessary to get the job done. **That willingness is a force**.

It's been said that the moment you totally commit yourself providence moves with you and all sorts of things occur to help you that might never otherwise have occurred. In psychological terms, commitment enables us to focus our creative energies on what we want to do while inhibiting the potential for competing responses and freeing us from indecision, distraction and negativity.

In Chapters 14 and 16, I describe working with the Canadian team at the 1983 Pan-American Games in Caracas, Venezuela. One of the teams I was involved with had the formidable challenge of having to win the gold medal in order to qualify for the 1984 Olympics in Los Angeles. The belief of the president of the sporting association was that if they didn't win they would lose funds vital to the support of their program. He felt that they had the talent and coaching to win. However, they had never won the gold medal before, so he asked me to help them to develop the necessary winning attitude.

I traveled with the team for a month working on the basics. Then I addressed their beliefs and their commitment directly. At a training camp about a month before the games, I asked the players to read the following "Statement of Intent."

"IT IS MY INTENTION TO WIN A GOLD MEDAL AT THE PAN-AMERICAN GAMES IN VENEZUELA THIS AUGUST. _____

I, _____, AM WILLING TO CONTRIBUTE WHATEVER IS NECESSARY TO SERVE THIS TEAM AND ITS SUCCESS IN ACHIEVING THAT GOAL.

I, _____, GENUINELY BELIEVE THAT WE ARE WINNERS AND THAT WE CAN AND WILL WIN IT ALL IN VENEZUELA.

THERE IS NOTHING TO PREVENT US FROM ACHIEVING OUR GOAL OF A GOLD MEDAL IN VENEZUELA. _____

I, _____, AM COMMITTING MYSELF TO SERVING THE TEAM AND WINNING THE GOLD MEDAL IN THE PAN-AMERICAN GAMES."

Each person was asked to read the five statements carefully. If they agreed with what was written, they were asked to sign the statement. Every player signed his statement. Next, each player was asked to read the statement aloud in front of his peers. Their teammates were asked to listen and comment on whether or not the reader sounded convincing in his commitment to the team's success. If he didn't, he was asked to reread the statement again ... and again, until his teammates were impressed. The athletes had a good deal of fun with the exercise and all succeeded in impressing their peers.

When the camp broke up, everyone was clear that the team's mission was to win the gold medal. And everyone was committed to making it happen. As a parting request, the players were asked to memorize the statement so that the next time we met, three weeks later, each individual would be able to recite the statement to the group "by heart."

When we met in Toronto on our way to Caracas three weeks later, all the players had memorized the mission statement. For the next three weeks before each team meeting, one player was randomly selected and asked to reiterate our intention and commitment.

The ritual of starting a meeting with the "by heart" recitation of the statement of intent became a meaningful, inspiring and entertaining reaffirmation of purpose. It was fun to be positive. Some of the players wrote the statement on the walls of their rooms. Everyone seemed committed to winning. And the team performed like they were committed. They won the first six games, and in so doing, qualified for the gold medal game against Argentina. Argentina was the perennial gold medalist. Amazingly, it had never lost a *single game* in Pan-American competition.

There was some tension before the big game. I recall two of the Team Canada players getting entangled in a shoving match that almost led to blows. I stepped in between them and said, "Remember you committed to doing whatever is necessary to serve the team. This doesn't serve the team." They both agreed immediately and changed channels.

The gold medal game was a battle. It could have gone either way. Actually, Argentina dominated the play. But Canada won the game and the gold. After the gold medal ceremony, the president of the association came over to congratulate me. "You know, Saul," he said. "It wasn't that they played any better than before. It's just that they didn't believe they could lose." I agreed. "They were committed to winning," I said with a grin.

3. Mental Toughness. Vince Lombardi said, "Mental toughness is essential to success."

Bobby Knight said, "Mental toughness is to the physical as four is to one."

Dave "Tiger" Williams said, "Mental toughness is playing like your next effort might be the difference. It's playing like your next effort after that might be the difference. It's playing like every effort you make throughout the game might be the difference. And it's doing it game after game."

Watching a Los Angeles Rams practice, George Meneffee, the Rams' trainer for the past thirty-five years, said, "The players today aren't as tough as they used to be. They may be bigger and faster … but they're not as mentally tough," When I asked George what he meant, he said, "In the old days, the same man played offense, defense, special teams … and he would play hurt, with no complaints. Today, if a player twists his ankle, he consults with his agent about whether or not it's in his career interest to practice."

I was talking to a group of Canadian women springboard and platform divers about mental training. "It's really very simple," I said. "All that's involved is having a clear idea of what you want to do ... and then doing it. Of course, sometimes something can come between the image and the action."

"Thirty-three feet of air," piped up a seventeen-year-old ten-meter diver. Mental toughness is leaping out into thirty-three feet of air and hitting the water at fifty-five miles per hour."

Six months later, the same diver called me from Winnipeg. She had won a gold medal in the Canadian ten-meter diving championship and was competing in the World Championships.

"How are you doing?" I asked.

"Not very well," Paige replied.

"What's happening?"

"I'm very nervous."

"What are you thinking? What are you saying to yourself as you dive?"

"Well, I tried telling myself it wasn't competition. I thought that if I said to myself that it was just practice I wouldn't be as nervous," she continued. "But it doesn't seem to work."

"It doesn't work because it's not true," I commented. "It is competition."

"When do you dive next?" I asked.

"In less than an hour."

"How many dives will you do?"

"Four," replied Paige.

"Do you know what they are?"

"Sure," she answered. "They're my optionals."

"What's the first dive?" I asked.

"It's an inward two-and-a-half pike."

"Okay. What do you have to do to really excel at that dive?" I asked. "Tell me three things … A, B, C."

"Well, I have to have a good takeoff … to go up and not out. That's A. Then I want to do a very tight pike … that's like a very tight somersault. That's B. And I have to focus on the water and have a clean entry. That's C."

"Then that's what you want to focus on. A, B, C," I said. "No matter what's happening or what you may be feeling, before that dive think and imagine A, B, C." Then we moved on to the next dive, and the third. With each dive I helped her define an A, B, C to focus on.

I advised her not to think of the second dive until she had completed the first. "Keep it simple. Think A, B, C for the dive you're doing. And that's it. If you feel nervous, or frightened, if you feel like you'd rather be at home … or somewhere else, don't fight it. Just breathe, release and "clear the screen." Then tune into your A, B, C for that dive." I went on, "You may be one of the younger competitors, but you're smart. You're talented. You're well coached. You've trained hard. And you are mentally tough."

Then we returned to the first dive. "Now, how well can you score on the first dive?" I asked.

"Eight and a half," Paige replied, describing a score out of ten.

"Okay." I asked, "What do you have to do to achieve an eight and a half out of ten?"

"I have to hit my A, B, C," she replied.

"Exactly. And that's what to focus on," I said. "The other feelings will be there. But you're mentally tough. You can tune them out. Focus on the A, B, C."

She did. And that afternoon, Paige moved up six places in the competition.

Two months later Paige called from Montreal. This time she was competing for a spot on Canada's Pan-American team. Like many auditions and job interviews, national team trials can be highly stressful events where a large number of people compete for a very limited number of places. Many competitors feel that the trials are more stressful than the actual games. There are three different diving events in international competition. There's the one-meter springboard, the three-meter springboard and the ten-meter tower. Quite unusually, Paige was competing in all three events.

Paige was leading the one-meter competition when she and three other experienced divers were disqualified because of an administrative technicality. It seems that there had been a change in the rules as to how the divers were to select their program and Paige and the others, including a former Olympian, had filled in their lists inappropriately.

Paige was very upset when she called. I allowed her to express her upset and to release some of the frustration and disappointment she was experiencing. We talked about the unfairness of it all. An official had reviewed her list the night before and said it was okay. Wasn't this about selecting the best team to represent the country? Why was their no appeal? She knew about the rule change and she should have known better. Why hadn't her coach spotted the error? And what about the coach who initiated the dispute just to give his diver a better chance? It really wasn't fair. ... Then we got into the fear. Now there was more pressure. What if it affected her three-meter performance the following day? What if she didn't win a spot on the team? What if ...?

After a few minutes, I asked Paige, "Are you the diver or the protestor?"

"I'm the diver," she replied.

"What's your next event?"

"Three meters."

"When is it?"

"Tomorrow."

"What's your first dive?"

"It's a simple forward dive."

"What do you have to do to do that well? What are the A, B, C's?"

"A is doing a very high takeoff. B is tucking and kicking." Paige continued, "C is a flat bodyline with a very clear entry."

"What's the next dive after that?"

Again she replied and we defined the A, B, C's.

Again she expressed her concern about the added pressure.

"You're a very good diver," I said. "You can handle it. Besides, the best antidote to pressure is to take a breath and focus on the A, B, C's for each dive."

The next day she called to say that she won the three-meter competition. After sharing her excitement, she expressed some concern that the ten-meter competition she was involved in later that day was almost anticlimactic. Having made the team, she wondered if the lack of pressure would affect her performance. Once again, I encouraged her to breathe, clear the screen of any nonproductive thoughts and focus on her A, B, C's for each dive. Later that day, she called to let me know that she had just won the ten-meter championship.

"Thanks," she said. "I don't know if I could have done it without you."

"You did it because you're a good diver, because you are mentally tough and because you are able to focus on the positive … on your A, B, C's."

Diving can be scary. Diving in the World Championships or in Pan-American or Olympic tryouts can be especially frightening. The same process that can help a young diver become mentally tougher and focus on her A, B, C's can help anyone cope more effectively with life's challenges.

Chuck Noll, the Pittsburg Steeler football coach, put it very nicely when he said, "Someplace along in life you are going to have to function in a pressure situation, and if you can learn to do it in a game where the results are not life and death, you can come to a situation where it is life and death and can be better able to cope."*

Mental toughness is fundamental in dealing effectively with pressure. It means staying tuned into the power channel ... no matter what. Mental toughness is not a magical property given by the gods to a select few. It can be developed by anyone with training.

Remember, whatever stimulus you focus on is magnified in your consciousness while the other stimuli competing for your attention are diminished in your perceptual field. That is, if you focus on difficulty and worry instead of on the task at hand, difficulty and worry become magnified in your consciousness. If you focus on the negative consequences of not being successful, the negative consequences seem to grow larger and become more significant. In contrast, if you focus on your power and your possibility, you empower yourself and you are better able to perform and persevere.

Mental toughness is about staying tuned into the power channel. It's practicing the techniques described in this book. Mental toughness is releasing distractions ... breathing easily ... and refocusing on thoughts, images, words and feelings that give you power. It's remembering that you are the boss and regardless of circumstances you control what you tune into on your mental TV.

---

*Quoted in Ferguson, Howard (ed.). *The Edge*. Getting The Edge Co.: Cleveland, Ohio, 1983.

Growing a winning attitude is a process of strengthening and integrating your motivation and commitment, as well as developing your ability to change channels and use the situation at hand — instead of allowing it to use you. As you do these things, your self-esteem will grow, and your perception of yourself and what is possible for you will grow with it.

4. Love is another quality of a winning attitude, and it's one that is often overlooked.

Love and fear are the two base emotions. They color our feelings and our lives. Either we love or we fear in everything we do. Love is an empowering, energizing and enabling force. In contrast, fear can be exhausting and limiting ... especially when it is experienced over an extended period of time. One of the real keys to performing under pressure is developing your ability to transform fear into love.

As I've said throughout the book, many people react to intense pressure by tightening up and contracting. The feeling state that usually accompanies contraction is fear. Often the fear is related to and stimulates negative thoughts: thoughts of what could go wrong?, what are the consequences? and what if ...?

At the beginning of the book, I described a batter stepping up to the plate in a high-pressure, critical last-out situation in the World Series. There's no doubt that he was feeling the pressure. Releasing some of that tension and fear and shifting his thinking from "Don't be the last out" and "I've *got* to get a hit" ... to "I *love* to hit the ball" is the kind of in-the-moment reaction shift that generates power and enhances performance dramatically. Winning attitudes develop as we consistently respond to pressure situations with love rather than fear.

Peter was an intelligent, skilled athlete with leadership potential who was prone to emotional outbursts that limited his impact. He was most inclined to lose control in high-pressure situations, especially late in the game. He rarely started an incident, but if provoked by an opponent he would retaliate thoughtlessly or antagonize an official who he felt had missed a call. The result was that he appeared to play with a good deal less intelligence than he was capable of, with indifference and with less than a winning attitude.

The truth was quite the contrary. Peter had the motivation of a winner. He was a perfectionist with very high standards and an intense desire to excel. What sparked his outbursts was frustration when his image of what *should* be didn't match what was. He was particularly critical of himself. And he was upset when others, opponents and officials, performed inappropriately (what to his mind was not according to the rules) and in a manner that prevented him from excelling.

Peter played on the edge ... with desperation and without a sense of loving himself. "The interesting thing," I explained to him, "is that when you play with fear instead of love, the game is no longer a challenge. Instead, it becomes a matter of survival. That's because your sense of who you are is threatened. If you don't perform well, then you feel you've failed ... and that you are not okay. When you play with fear, everything becomes more stressful and exhausting. It's a drain. In contrast, when you play with love you are freer. You have more power. The game is more fun. You can play better, with more awareness and control ... and you play better longer."

I went on to say, "We all have fear. Fear is a quality of being alive. The question is, how can you transform some of your fear into love? And in your case, Peter, how do you balance your intense desire to excel and your high standards with a little self-love?

"Part of the answer lies in some very simple techniques that will bring you more balance and awareness to the moment. Breathing is one. Just taking time as you breathe for the inbreath to come all the way in ... and for the outbreath to go all the way out is a simple, powerful way of loving yourself. It will give you the sense that there's more time. It's centering. And it's empowering."

I demonstrated the breathing keys. Then I showed Peter how to relate his breathing to simple power thoughts and images. "You get more of what you think about," I said, "As you play, it's important for you to acknowledge yourself repeatedly. Tell yourself that you're okay, that you're working hard and that you are doing a good job. Instead of focusing on an unsuccessful end result, like a pass you or your teammate may have missed, or a bad call by an official, and re-acting to that, focus on your incessant hustle and your ability to move the play forward. Throughout the game, take a breath, ac-knowledge yourself, think about what you do well, say to yourself, 'way to work.' Acknowledge the situation. Think, 'I love the chal-lenge.'"

We discussed a variety of game situations from the perspective of Peter *having* to make something happen and playing with a survival mentality. Then we ran through the same game situations with Peter imaging himself playing with greater confidence and control.

I explained to Peter why his previous attitude made him vulner-able to nonproductive emotional outbursts. "When you are playing with an attitude of fear, the game is a matter of survival. It's like a war. There is no margin for error. Every opponent is a threat to you. When they get in your way, you feel like killing them. When you make a mistake, your thinking becomes self-destructive. When an official misses a call, you direct your anger at him. The emotions generated by this mindset are unbalancing and exhausting. They lower your game intelligence and they bring you down.

"On the other hand, if you're playing with an attitude of self-love, your mind-state and your reactions will be more centered and balanced. Sure, the game may be tough and challenging, that's why you play. When you address it with love, 'I love the challenge,' the exercise will become more fulfilling. The drive to excel is both empowered and controlled with love. Self-love insulates people from playing with desperation. And contrary to what some coaches may lead you to believe, desperation is not a high-performance mind-state. Acknowledge your drive and hustle. Loving yourself will allow you to be more flexible. It will help you to react more easily and efficiently."

As we were in the middle of the season, I wanted to leave Peter with some simple and very practical advice, something he could use during a game. I encouraged him to repeatedly tune into his breathing throughout the game and to acknowledge himself by using three power thoughts. The first two acknowledged him for who he was and for his hustling style of play. They were "I'm okay" and "way to work." The last addressed the challenge provided by any and every situation. It was simply, "I love it."

I HURT AND I HATE. The observations I have been making about love and fear are by no means limited to sport. They exist in every theater of human experience ... and most especially where human beings are challenged. For the past two years, I've been working with people who have been injured and who are experiencing a great deal of chronic pain. Some of the techniques I use in working with them involve breathing, releasing and refocusing. As they learn to make use of these techniques, many of them are able to significantly reduce the intensity of their discomfort. Increasingly, I've observed that the greatest gains in pain control seem to come when people are able to shift their mindset from the fear and anger they've been experiencing to love.

In the course of our working together, I often ask my clients to go into their plain and to explore it. As part of the process, I ask them, "If you were able to talk to your pain, what would you say to it?" Most reply that they are angry with the pain and that they want to get rid of it, to turn it off, cut it out, beat it up, kill it and even shoot it. Their response is hardly surprising when you consider that the pain is often the number one thing that they focus on and attribute to destroying their pleasure of life and eroding their sanity.

One thing I do is ask them to relax ... then go into the pain. I encourage them to "love the part of you that hurts." I explain that anger and fear cause tension, dis-ease and more pain, while love leads to ease and has a greater potential for regeneration. I encourage them to channel any anger they feel into mobilizing change and to resist directing it inward ... or at others. I explain to them, "If you love that part of you that hurts, as you ease into it, you will be able to stream energy through it, and in so doing some positive and painless changes may begin to take place. On the other hand, if you fight that part of you that hurts, the result is usually more tension, more pressure and more pain." The people who seem to make the greatest changes are those who can transform their fear to love.

A final message for creating a winning attitude, one that will allow you to cope more effectively with life's pressures and pains, is to **love yourself**. It's a context and a catalyst for breathing, releasing and refocusing. And it allows the process to work for you.

CHAPTER 17 TRAINING NOTES

A Winning Attitude

1. **Week one:** At least once a day, every day, stand in front of a mirror, look at yourself and say (aloud),

   "I'm okay."
   "I am a multi-talented individual."
   "I deserve to express my abilities."
   "I make a difference."

2. **Week two:** Make a want list. Write down twenty-five things you want to do, feel, be or accomplish.

3. **Week three:** Create clear, meaningful goals. Define two goals in each of the following categories: health, relationship, career, material and recreational. Make a commitment to realize one goal from each of the above categories in the next three months.

4. **Week four:** Create an action plan you are willing to follow to achieve your goals. Write down some power thoughts and images that will support you on your way.

   For each goal, script out three situations where circumstances and self-doubt could lead to you creating some negative feelings, thoughts and images. In each case, write down what the limiting feelings, thoughts and images might be. Then change channels and imagine yourself tuning into some feelings, thoughts and images that will empower you.

Every day, acknowledge and affirm:

"I am a positive and powerful human being."
"I have a clear sense of direction ... A, B, C."
"I am mentally tough."
"I control the switch."
"I'm okay."

LIVING IT

chapter eighteen

A
HIGH-PERFORMANCE
LIFESTYLE

———

In writing *Performing Under Pressure*, I wanted to communicate the simplest components that would have the greatest impact on enhancing your ability to perform under pressure.

There are a number of factors that are also extremely important in nurturing your ability to perform under pressure. One of them is *lifestyle*.

For several years, whenever I spoke to business groups across North America, I would ask the audience two questions. Question One: which factors have most contributed to your success? Question Two: What (if anything) could limit your continued growth and success?

The three most frequent responses to the first question were:

1. positive attitude
2. hard work
3. surrounding myself with positive, talented,
   hard-working people.

In answering the second question (what could limit your continued growth and success?) their overwhelming response was a factor that is rarely given any training time or attention in performance enhancement seminars. It was *health*.

People are increasingly becoming aware that if they are sick they won't perform very well. And they're becoming more conscious of some of the basic ingredients that nurture health and consistent high-level performance. The list includes:

1. diet
2. exercise
3. recreation
4. relaxation
5. relationships
6. a healthy perspective.

We don't live in a vacuum. We live in a biochemical, psycho-physical, socio-economic lifespace. Our ability to concentrate, handle stress, think clearly and excel under pressure is directly affected by how we live in this space. **What you eat, your exercise, recreational, rest and social patterns all have a profound effect on how you express yourself in the game of life.**

DIET

Eat to Be a Consistent Winner

The nervous system operates on biochemical impulses. What you eat becomes your biochemistry and can impact on your stress tolerance, your ability to change channels and the quality of your programing.

The standard American diet is high in fat, high in protein and high in sugar. While a burger, fries and a Coke may appeal to some people's taste buds and nurture short-term "start-stop" living, in the long run it's stressful to the organism, and the environment. Over time, it reduces health and performance and increases your vulnerability to stress and dis-ease.

Like most experts, I advise a diet that is:

1. **High is complex carbohydrates**
   About sixty-five percent of your diet should consist of these foods. That means a significant amount of unrefined cereal grain, vegetables and fruits.

2. **Low in fat**
   The American Heart Association recommends that we limit our fat intake to thirty-five percent of our diet. That is simply not rigorous enough for proactive health care. Unless you're an Eskimo, I'd suggest that the fat content of your diet not exceed twenty percent. A simple guideline is: if it looks, feels and tastes greasy, if it's fried or smothered in butter, avoid it.

3. **Moderate in protein**
   Most North Americans could cut their protein intake by a third. Look for alternatives to animal protein. I used to say to

people, "You don't need to eat meat every day." Now I say,
"It's a health risk to be eating meat every day."

4. **Relatively free from refined sugars**

   Cookies, candy, cakes and Cokes are an unhealthy habit and
   an addictive one. They appeal entirely to one's sense of taste.
   Artificial sweeteners aren't much better. (Most of them have
   been shown to have significant side effects.) Simple sugars are
   the fuel of the nervous system. Refined sugars can be unbalancing and stressful. If you want something sweet, eat fruit.

5. **Sensible**

   Choose simple preparations of wholesome foods as opposed
   to foods that are highly processed and loaded with chemical
   additives. And avoid overeating.

Avoid Drugs

I can't think of a faster way to lose control of the switch than by "doing
drugs." Yet, the use of drugs, prescription or otherwise, for both stimulation and to reduce stress and dis-ease is epidemic* in our culture.

---

*If you don't think there's a super-push to perform or that drugs aren't
epidemic in our culture, you might consider this: in 1984, Dr. Robert
Goldman asked 198 world-class athletes, "Would you take a pill that
would guarantee you a gold medal even if you knew it would kill you in
five years?" One hundred and three said they would.

Also, in 1984 some members of the U.S. Olympic cycling team practiced
blood doping. That's a process whereby blood is taken from a competitor
a couple of months before a race. Following a natural replenishment, the
removed blood is injected into the athlete prior to competition, giving him
or her a surplus of red blood cells. In the case of a couple of the U.S.
cyclists, they didn't have sufficient time to replenish their own stocks, so
they simply went to the blood bank and got someone else's.

A 1989 survey reported in *USA Today* indicated that approximately
seven percent of high school boys in the U.S. had taken steroids either to
enhance their athletic ability or their appearance.

If you're looking for enhanced or altered states, develop your ability to release, breathe, and focus. Remember, the "response-ability" is yours. Looking to drugs to support the effect you want will ultimately result in dependancy, a loss of power ... and more *stress*.

EXERCISE INTELLIGENTLY

An excellent way to increase your resistance to stress is to exercise, and to stay in good physical shape. One of the best ways to get into shape is to move around. People are made to move. Exercise, movement and action all stimulate energy flow. They are a balance to too much "sitting and thinking" or watching TV or a computer terminal. Walking, jogging, cycling, dancing and swimming are all fine. Action games like racquetball and tennis are also fine, provided you don't take them too seriously.

Most experts recommend a minimum of three to four twenty-minute periods of accelerated movement each week. Along with aerobic movement, some "stretching" and "strengths" are also advisable. One of the keys to intelligent exercise is to avoid making your exercise sessions too violent, especially if you haven't been working out regularly. Overdoing it can result in more stress and breakdown than exercise prevents. I have seen far too many people who have injured legs and backs by jogging excessively on hard pavement. But the data is in, and the results are crystal clear: **exercising intelligently and consistently** at something you enjoy will enhance your ability to handle pressure and stress.

EXPERIENCE QUALITY RECREATION

To re-create means to re-new. Think of things that you do that renew you, that *give* you energy. They may include sport, exercise, playing music, painting, dancing, cooking, reading, listening to music, being with people, conversing, being close, or being alone, being quiet or meditating. You are response-able for creating healthy recreational habits. Do things regularly that are energizing, balancing and that you enjoy. Enjoyment adds life and energy to the process.

Television is North America's most common form of entertainment. However, it's not true recreation. For most people, it's more of a diversion or escape from the stresses and pressures of life than anything that's energizing or recharging. Cultivate recreational patterns that renew you.

RELAX

The word "relax" means to regain a natural feeling of looseness and ease. As such, relaxation is the perfect balance to tension and disease. It's a mind-body process that promotes health, healing and longevity. Relaxation addresses all systems. It improves respiratory efficiency. It lowers heart rate and blood pressure. It reduces muscle tension. And it balances the activity of the left and right cerebral hemispheres of the brain.

In this book, I describe in some detail how to relax your breathing, how to relax different muscle groups in the body and how to tune out worry and negative thoughts that increase tension and stress. In reality, these are not separate elements. They all blend together. As you tune into your breathing, allow your body to relax. As your body relaxes, it becomes easier to breathe. As you breathe more easily, your mind becomes more centered and calm. As the mind calms, the body relaxes.

Relaxation is one of the keys to a high-performance lifestyle. Incorporate your knowledge of relaxation into your life. Experience it in its most simple form as the breathe ... release ... refocus technique, or as twenty connected breaths. Take a two- to three-minute "power break" a couple of times during the day. Have a ten-minute "relaxation time out" at a low energy point in your day. The thing to remember is that relaxing is energizing, recharging, balancing and it feels good.

DEVELOP EMPOWERING RELATIONSHIPS

The second most frequent response to the question of what (if anything) could limit your continued growth and success was *"negativity."* A tremendous drain on anyone's personal energy is working, living and performing with negative people.

Like our health, the social context in which we live and perform can be nurturing or inhibiting. Whenever possible, create relationships that are supportive, positive and that empower you. Seek out winners, positive people who look to the potential and the possibility that lies within us all. If possible, avoid people who are negative and destructive. They are a limiting stress. If it's your reality to live and work with negative, destructive people, use the experience as an opportunity to develop more psycho-physical control, to release … breathe … and stay tuned into the power and possibility channel. Take from their message what is useful; be willing to communicate and work at being less attached to their approval.

You cannot always control the circumstances in your life, but you are response-able to control your reactions to them. Part of learning how to succeed in the face of a meaningful challenge is maintaining that kind of healthy perspective.

If there's a single concluding thought, it's that winners **enjoy** the challenge and the opportunity to excel … as well as the pressure that goes with it.

THE *PERFORMING UNDER PRESSURE* TRAINING SCHEDULE

In 1988, I worked with the U.S. wrestling team in preparation for the Olympic Games. The Greco-Roman coach was Pavel Katsen, a Russian who had been trained in coaching at one of the leading sport institutes in the Soviet Union. One of the things that impressed me about Pavel, along with his great enthusiasm, was the training schedule he developed for the team. It described precisely what should be done on several parameters (strength, aerobic capacity and actual wrestling training) day after day for a period of two months leading up to the Olympics. Training in each area was programed to increase diversity and decrease "burnout," with training levels rising and falling and calculated to peak just prior to the Olympic Games.

Performing Under Pressure includes a four-week training schedule that outlines specific breathing, release and focusing techniques. It defines when and how to work with them to increase performance and wellbeing.

FOUR-WEEK
TRAINING PROGRAM

ELEMENTS KEY

a. breathing 1. rhythm
2. inspiration
3. continuity

b. release 1. tension release
2. scanning
3. streaming
4. blowing it off

c. focusing/programing 1. power thoughts
2. winning imagery
3. feelings of competence

TIMING

WEEK ONE (every day)

a. 10-minute breathing session .... focus a:1*

2–3 times a day, 6 breaths .... focus a:1

b. 5-minute tension release .... focus b:1

c. 8–10 power thoughts .... focus c:1

WEEK TWO (every day)

a. 10-minute breathing session .... focus a:1+2

2–3 times a day, 6 breaths .... focus a:2

b. 2–3 minutes/day, scanning, releasing, streaming .... focus b: 1, 2,+3

c. power thoughts, revise & repeat .... focus c:1

imagery, script elements .... focus c:2

feelings: define winning feelings .... focus c:3

WEEK THREE (every day)

a. 10-minute breathing session .... focus a:1, 2,+3

2–3 times a day, 20 "connected breaths" .... focus a:3

b. 3–4 times/day, 30 seconds, scan, release, breathe, stream ...focus b:2+3

3 times/day, blow off tension 1–10 drill .... focus b:4

c. power thoughts, revise & tape .... focus c:1

imagery, 5 minutes/day, ease & effect .... focus c:2

3+ times/day, 2–5 second "highlights" .... focus c:2

feelings, on awakening, feeling for the day .... focus c:3

---

*See Elements Key

WEEK FOUR (every day)

a. 10-minute breathing session ....focus a:1, 2, 3,+b:3

    2–3 times/day, 6 breaths ....focus a:1 +2

    2–3 times/day, 20 connected breaths ....focus a:3

b. 3–4 times/day, 30 seconds –1 minute, scan, release,

       breathe, stream ....focus b:2+3

    3 times/day, blow off tension, 1–10 drill, optional punch ....focus b:4

c. power thoughts, revise and repeat ....focus c:1

    imagery, 5 minutes/day, imagery performing with

       ease & effectiveness ....focus c:2

    3–4 times/day, image 2–5-second highlights ....focus c:2

    feelings, create and recreate winning feelings ....focus c:3

EVERY DAY ... AND WHENEVER POSSIBLE:

Combine Thoughts, Feelings, Images with Breathing & Release.

WEEK ONE (every day)

FOCUS

THINK

Create 8–10 power thoughts. Pair a thought with a feeling. Repeat your power thoughts several times a day in association with your breathing and release (Chapter 15).

BREATHE

10-minute breathing session daily

Focus on breathing rhythm.

2–3 times a day take 6 breaths (Chapter 4).

"I'm the boss."

"The boss takes his/her time."

"I deserve my time."

"There's power in rhythm."

RELEASE

Every day take 5 minutes to tense and release 6 muscle groups (Chapter 9).

"I control the switch."

"I can release in any part of my body."

"I deserve to feel good."

LIFESTYLE (Weeks One and Two)

Exercise at least 15 minutes a day 3 times a week.
Reduce the fat and sugar content of your diet.
Experience a 10-minute relaxation break every day (Chapter 19).

WEEK TWO (every day)

Thought and breath work together. As you breathe, remember to think thoughts that empower you and give you pleasure.

BREATHE

Take a 10-minute breathing session each day.

2–3 times a day, take 6 breaths, focus on your breathing rhythm and the inspiration.

Repeatedly throughout the day, inspire yourself (Chapter 5).

THINK

Add a new power thought to your list each week.

"I inspire myself."

"I have a personal connection to an unlimited supply of energy."

RELEASE

Spend 2–3 minutes as part of your daily breathing session scanning, releasing and streaming energy out to the 5 points (Chapters 9 & 10).

"Energy flows to me ...
and through me."

IMAGERY

Script out the specific elements that you want to imagine and mentally rehearse. Write them down.

Spend at least 4–5 minutes each day imagining yourself performing with ease, power and effectiveness (Chapter 14).

"The mind is like a TV set that watches one program at a time. And you control the switch."

"I enjoy experiencing myself as successful."

"I deserve to express all my ability" (Chapter 15).

FEELINGS

Become clear about the exact feelings that you want to experience.
Determine the ones that facilitate you. Create a feeling script. Write
down those feelings and the circumstances under which you've created
them. Develop as clear a picture as possible about the specific feelings
(ease, power, competence and confidence) that you want to experience
under pressure. Spend 3 minutes twice a day practicing creating these
feelings (Chapter 16).

WEEK THREE (every day)

BREATHE

In your 10-minute breathing
session, pay attention to the wave
after wave quality of the breath.

2–3 times a day, take 20
"connected breaths." As you do,
think of your breathing: as turning
the wheel, as waves in the ocean
(Chapter 6).

THINK

"The breath is an endlessly turning
wheel.
"The wheel keeps turning."

"The waves never stop."
"They can wash anything away."
"The force is with me."

RELEASE

3–4 times a day, take 30 seconds
to a minute to scan, release and
breathe. Stream energy through
your body, especially when you
feel tense, tired, depressed or sore
(Chapters 9 & 10).

"I'm the master of my reactions.
I'm the boss."

"Energy flows to me ... and
through me."
"I deserve to feel good."

BLOWING OFF TENSION

Here's an excellent disinhibiting and energizing exercise to practice every day. Find a place where you won't be disturbing anyone. Then count out loud from 1 to 10. Begin with 1 being moderately loud and increase the loudness and intensity with each number so that you are *roaring* on numbers 7 to 10. Repeat this process 3 times (Chapter 11).

IMAGERY

Spend 5 minutes a day imagining yourself performing with ease and effectiveness.

First, imagine excelling relaxed, then under pressure.

Throughout the day, run 2–5-second highlights of yourself performing with power and ease. Before an important event, release … breathe … and run a winning highlight (Chapter 14).

THINKING

Put these thoughts on a tape recorder and listen to them throughout the day whenever you have a free ear (Chapter 15).

"The mind is like a TV …"

"You control the switch."

"I get more of what I think about."

"Repetition builds strength."

WEEK FOUR (every day)

BREATHE

In your 10-minute breathing session, experience rhythm, inspiration and the wave after wave quality of the breath (Chapters 4–6).

2–3 times a day, take 6 breaths, focus on rhythm and inspiration.

2–3 times a day, take 20 "connected breaths." As you do, think of your breathing as turning the wheel, as waves in the ocean.

THINK

"The breath is like waves in the ocean."

"The waves never rush."

"The waves never stop."

"The wheel keeps turning."

"The force is with me."

RELEASE

3–4 times a day, take 30 seconds to a minute to scan, release and breathe.
Stream energy through your body, especially when you feel tense, tired, depressed or sore (Chapters 9 & 10).

"I'm the master of my reactions. I'm the boss."

"Energy flows to me … and through me.

"I deserve to feel good."

BLOWING OFF TENSION

Optional: As you go up the loudness/intensity scale from 1 to 10, you can punctuate each number with a (safe) punch. What's important is to keep increasing the amplitude of your sound and your intensity. Do at least 3 repetitions a day (Chapter 11).

IMAGERY

Spend 5 minutes a day imagining yourself performing with ease and effectiveness. First, imagine excelling relaxed. Then, under pressure.

Just like last week, run 2–5-second highlights of yourself performing with power and ease throughout the day.

Before an important event, release ... breathe ... and image a winning highlight (Chapter 14).

THINKING

Continuously refine and repeat your power thoughts.

"The mind is like a TV ..."

"It's my TV. I control the switch."

"Creative thought is one of the most powerful forces on the planet ... and I am the thinker" (Chapter 15).

FEELINGS

Every morning on awakening, spend a moment releasing and breathing ... then think of a feeling that you will bring to mind to facilitate you and give you a lift all day long.
Throughout the day, bring that feeling to mind.
Experience it.

Begin to consciously practice changing your feelings from tension to ease by breathing, releasing and redirecting your energy before reacting.

As you do, think:

"I'm the boss. I control my physical and mental reactions. I deserve to feel good. I control the switch on my mental TV. I deserve to express all my abilities" (Chapter 16).

LIFESTYLE

Exercise at least 20 minutes a day 4 times a week. Movement and exercise are a great way to de-stress, balance systems and tone the organism. It's quality recreation.

Reduce the fat and sugar content of your diet even more. Moderate your protein intake.

Experience a 10-minute relaxation break every day. In addition, and more importantly, practice releasing, breathing, refocusing and recharging throughout the day (at least a dozen times) (Chapter 19).

Be clear and positive.

Be kind to yourself and others.